LANDSCAPE ILLUSTRATIONS

OF THE

BIBLE,

VOL. I.

Drawn by J. D. Harding from a sketch by Will'm John Bankes Esq.   Engraved by E. Finden.

ENTRANCE TO PETRA. — EDOM.

JEREM. XLIX. 17.

LANDSCAPE ILLUSTRATIONS

OF

THE BIBLE,

CONSISTING OF

VIEWS OF THE MOST REMARKABLE PLACES

MENTIONED IN

The Old and New Testaments.

FROM ORIGINAL SKETCHES TAKEN ON THE SPOT

ENGRAVED BY W. AND E. FINDEN.

WITH

DESCRIPTIONS

BY

THE REV. THOMAS HARTWELL HORNE, B.D.

OF ST. JOHN'S COLLEGE, CAMBRIDGE, AUTHOR OF " AN INTRODUCTION TO THE STUDY
OF THE HOLY SCRIPTURES," ETC.

IN TWO VOLUMES.

VOL. I.

LONDON:

JOHN MURRAY, ALBEMARLE STREET.

SOLD ALSO BY CHARLES TILT, FLEET STREET.

MDCCCXXXVI.

First published in this edition in 1998 by
The R. S. Surtees Society
Manor Farm House,
Nunney, Nr. Frome, Somerset, BA11 4NJ, U.K.

ISBN 0 948560-31-2

Printed in Great Britain by
Antony Rowe Ltd,
Chippenham, Wiltshire

ACKNOWLEDGEMENTS

On behalf of the R. S. Surtees Society we would like to thank:—

Nadim Shahadi, Centre for Lebanese Studies, Oxford
Dom Philip Jebb, Downside Abbey, Somerset
Anthony Windrum, formerly Foreign & Commonwealth Office

Our workforce:

Mrs. J. Wright, Membership and Orders Secretary
Peter Merer, Despatch and General Interest

also

The Staff of the London Library; Castle Graphics, Nunney;
Antony Rowe Ltd., Chippenham; The Downside Abbey Bindery; The
Warminster Book Shop; March Press, Frome; The Fine Art Society,
148 New Bond Street, London, W.1.

and

Mr. and Mrs. E. Hasbani for their hospitality and knowledge,
past and present.

FOREWORD

Every adult in 19th century Britain had some kind of imagined picture of the landscape of the Holy Land. This vision might have been fanciful, and constructed of images furnished by the English countryside, so that the brook Kedron, flowing between Jerusalem and Mount Olivet, was imagined as a warmer version of a local willow-hung stream, and the cedars in the park of a great house stood in for the Cedars of Lebanon. Yet it did not matter, as any reminiscence of the places of the scriptures was seen as an aid to faith. After all, there were willows in the Holy Land too, and some of the exotic cedars were grown from seed sent from Mount Lebanon.

Virtually every one possessed this mental furniture; only in the very worst industrial slums were some children to be found who had as yet no idea of the Bible. Before the education acts of 1870, the bedrock of British educatioon had been the Bible, and even after that date religious assembly was obligatory in schools, whereas no other subject was legally compulsory.

Anyone with any education at all knew at least the names of many Biblical localities, which they had heard repeated endlessly in lessons and sermons in churches and chapels. The places of worship themselves had names given in remembrance of the Holy Land, such as the many chapels that were named, for example, Galilee, Sion, Bethel, in every town in Britain.

In the 19th century, the language of the people was still suffused with biblical references, conscious and unconscious. This is not surprising, given the supremely vigorous and poetic language of the Bible. That is, considering the magnificent language used by its 17th century English translators, in their renderings of the poetry and prose of the Authorised Version (started 1607, published 1611 at the command of King James I). It was literally the language of Shakespeare, who was writing his mature work in the same first decade of the 17th century. Then the English language was arguably at the height of its flexibility, vigour and directness, and some of this primitive vitality persisted into the 19th century. Even atheists, such as Shelley, and heretics, such as William Blake, could not escape its influence, as they too had been brought up on the Bible, Shakespeare and Milton, and in the midst of their rebellion were compelled to use the same language as their fellow countrymen in order to be understood.

Although the earnest middle classes of the 19th century, caught up in the evangelical revival, would be expected to refer constantly to the scriptures, the more worldly often mingled the characters of the Bible with references to classical mythology, often in a jocular and irreverent way. So a larger-than-life quintessentially Victorian soldier, traveller and author such as Fred Burnaby could casually refer to his sleeping cab driver as 'my Jehu in the arms of Morpheus' *(A Ride to Khiva)* and expect to be understood. It is unlikely that a modern school child would pick up the reference to Jehu, who 'driveth furiously' (2 Kings 9.20) and to the classical god of sleep, but such things were taken for granted in those days.

No matter how secular the occupation and interests of ordinary citizens, the Bible could not be entirely avoided. What appears to us now as the completely religion-free sports of horse racing and hunting did not escape. The most famous hunting correspondent of the time, C. J. Apperley, took the pseudonym of Nimrod 'the mighty hunter before the Lord' (Genesis 10.9). Even Surtees, whose themes and language in such novels as *Mr Sponge's Sporting Tour* are as colloquial and unbiblical as possibly could be, refers to the drunken groom Peter Leather as 'one of the fallen angels of servitude'.

Everyone knew of the Bible, and many were curious about the places mentioned in the scriptures, particularly as the explosion of travellers penetrating the East had already produced a good crop of first hand accounts of the holy places as they now appeared. (In the period between 1800 and 1878, a minimum of 2,000 authors published books on Palestine). Thus the publisher John Murray, already secure in the knowledge that there had been a large audience eager for an earlier publication illustrated by the Findens, decided to publish volumes devoted to the Landscape of the Bible. Given that in the 1830s there was a rapidly expanding literate public, who were mostly middle class churchgoers, and more desirous of respectability than their Regency forebears, it was a good choice. The only major problem was that of rival publications devoted to similar themes, trying to cash in at the same moment.

(Typical books issued in rivalry were John Carne's *Syria, The Holy Land, Asia Minor, &c, Illustrated,* Fisher, Son and Co., 1937–38, and the Revd Robert Walsh's *Constantinople and the Scenery of the Seven Churches of Asia Minor, Illustrated,* Fisher, Son & Co., 1838–40.)

Edward Francis Finden (1791–1857) and William Finden (1787–1852) were leading engravers of their time, working both independently and jointly, who contributed illustrations to numerous publications. By 1836 they were probably best known for their joint venture *Finden's Landscape & Portrait Illustrations to the Life and Works of Lord Byron in three volumes* 1833–4. published by John Murray, after which they published the plates to this book *Landscape Illustrations of the Bible,* 2 vols, 1836, with a text by the Revd T. H. Horne. After that their major production was *Finden's Royal Gallery of British Art,* 1838–49, which led, as we shall see, to financial difficulties.

These three books encapsulated the progress and contradictions of 19th century taste. The first book featured the wicked Regency hero, Lord Byron, dashing and romantic, still in vogue in the 1830s. The demand for the romantic pictures (often views in Italy and the Middle East) to accompany the poetry and drama of Byron's works suggested that was another, even bigger audience. This readership might not want the reprobate sceptical and pagan works, but instead might buy a book of romantic but harmless and improving pictures of the landscape of belief with a safer text. A child at Sunday School could be shown the images, even if they could not read or understand the words, and the most educated, pious and elderly would find the tasteful interpretations of the sketches of a Turner or David Roberts a useful accompaniment to belief.

Heady with the success of this publication, the Findens then tried the idea of marketing art pure and simple, in a third illustrated book, but although art later in the century almost replaced religion amongst certain intellectuals, the *Royal Gallery of British Art* never attracted such a devoted following. Art was then (and still is) one of the most contentious issues, and in the selections of artists and pictures, they had to make choices and take sides. The public, probably by then sated with a surfeit of illustrated books, did not buy the volumes in quantity, involving the Findens in heavy financial loss.

So the Findens started by exploiting Regency romanticism, which was becoming less respectable and less popular, went on to the certainties of the Biblical landscape (no questions of doctrine were at stake here), into the uncertain and often vexed question of Taste in Art. This subject, where even the best thinkers of the 19th century, such as John Ruskin, were lured into controversy and contradiction, nearly ruined the Findens.

However, it was not all plain sailing with *Landscape Illustrations of the Bible.* In 1832–33, Sir Augustus Wall Callcott, with William Turner, David Roberts, Clarkson Stanfield and James Duffield Harding, and other well-known and established artists were comissioned by John Murray to provide drawings for this series of prints illustrating Biblical scenery. Callcott in particular quarrelled with the Findens and wrote to Barry saying he was 'offended on finding I had to take what Mr Turner had relinquished'.

The thirty-seven or so artists, some of whom provided the initial sketches, and others who worked them up for the engravers to copy, were a very varied group. For example, they included Louis Cassas, a French painter and engraver who worked in Syria, Turkey, Egypt and the Lebanon, C. R. Cockerell the architect who had travelled as a young man on the grander tour of Greece, Turkey and the Holy Land, Frederick Catherwood, an architectural draughtsman who had drawn the antiquities of Egypt, Selina Bracebridge, an amateur who made watercolour sketches of her travels, and the diplomat and traveller James Morjer who was famous as the author of *The Adventures of Hajii Baba of Ispahan.*

Of course, most of the more famous artists had not actually been to the Holy Land, but were asked to use sketches from other travellers. Some of them were good artists in their own right, such as Sir Charles Barry, the future architect of the Houses of Parliament, who early in his career had made the on-the-spot sketch of Mount Moriah that Turner used for his drawing. Edward Finden used the 'Turnerised' sketch of Barry as the direct source for his etching. Other prints do not have quite such an illustrious pedigree. A most illuminating sequence is that leading up to the penultimate image entitled 'Sardis. One of the Seven Churches.'

It is worth examining this print in some detail for the light it casts on Victorian book illustration generally. The initial on-the-spot sketch by a 'Mr Maude' (whoever he was) still exists; it is in the Searight collection at the Victoria & Albert Museum. To tell the truth, it is a rather dull but competent amateur ink and wash sketch of the only two colums still standing of the Temple of Artemis, with no figures or anything of emotional interest. William Finden then gave Clarkson Stanfield this unprepossessing drawing to 'work up' and do his best with.

Sardis, now Sart in modern Turkey, was a desolate spot then, with only a few ruins as a pathetic remnant of the fabulous wealth of one of the Seven Churches of Asia admonished in the Apocalypse, the Revelation of St John the Divine. Presumably this sketch was the only authentic representation that the Findens could obtain. Stanfield duly used it as a the starting point of his own painting (also in the Searight Collection), but immediately made it into a dramatic watercolour, rivalling his contemporary John Martin, by introducing a thunderstorm and a rider who has been thrown down by his horse, panicked by the apocalyptic weather. The finished print in the book is a fairly faithful version of this dramatic improvement.

Thomas Clarkson Stanfield RA (1793–1867) was the son of the actor, J. F. Stanfield. He had spent his early career at sea, before he became a leading marine painter, and he painted stage scenery for theatres in London and Edinburgh, a close rival to David Roberts. He also painted dioramas and panoramas. Although the Findens desired authenticity, in that the basis of the finished illustration had a starting point based on some kind of reality (Mr Maude's pedestrian sketch), they expected an added artistic and dramatic dimension to stir the imagination of the readers. Judging by his previous career, Stanfield was the man for the job.

It was not merely a picture of some ruins; the image referred to the fulfilment of a Biblical prophecy which actually looked forward to the final days, the terrible moment of God's Last Judgement. Only an artist's imagination could transform Mr Maude's record drawing into a visual sermon.

The prints themselves are usually described generically as 'engravings' and the Findens as 'Engravers.' In fact the prints that they excelled in producing are mostly very fine etchings, a quicker and freer medium than the laborious technique of engraving, where one small image might take many weeks of intensive work. An engraver would incise the copper very slowly, forming an image by cutting into the surface of the metal with an engraving tool.

The etchers would also copy and interpret the image, but rapidly draw it with an etching needle through the wax resist on the copper plate, before the metal was plunged into a bath of acid, which would eat into the copper where the etching tool had cut through the film of wax. After the acid was washed away and the plate cleaned of the wax resist, the etched lines would then be filled with ink, and the rest of the plate wiped clean. A sheet of paper was placed on the plate, ready to pick up the ink from its etched lines, under the powerful force of the press.

It was still a slow and laborious process compared with modern methods of photo-mechanical printmaking, yet much faster (and cheaper) than engraving. Yet even in the hands of such skilled craftsmen as the Findens and their team of apprentices, the etching process could not quite match the very finest effects of engraving.

Many Victorians subsequently formed their mental pictures of the Holy Land on these small illustrations, modifying their imagined views of Jordan, Jerusalem and Bethlehem, which they had tentatively formed as they had listened to and then read the scriptures for themselves. The paradox is that the etchings are in black and white, and were not intended to be hand-coloured, so that the brilliant colours of the Stanfield sketch and the glories of Turner in the picture of Corinth had to be provided solely in the imagination of the readers. Now that the modern world is filled with complete colour images of every kind and size, it is hard to grasp and to remember that early Victorians saw relatively few illustrations in colour. Thus they had to rely solely on their imaginations to fill the gaps in a way, and to an extent that is difficult now to comprehend.

There was a keen appreciation of the fine details of the etchings, sharpened by the fact that illustrations of any kind were so few in comparison with our image-glutted age. As we now contemptuously throw away a junk-mail catalogue, we do not consider that we are disposing of perhaps a thousand individual high-resolution colour images. These cheap and disposable images would have astounded a Victorian illustrator who had laboured many hours to achieve just one reproductive image before the invention of reliable photo-mechanical reproduction.

The publication history of the *Landscape Illustrations* prints and the volumes that contained them is complicated. Like many Victorian books which had a large series of illustrations, they were issued first in parts, and then later republished as a two volume set, with various possible orders. Hence in some copies the plates are numbered differently from their actual sequence in the binding. This edition is published with the plates in the order that they are mentioned in the Bible, so that the beginning, a picture of Mount Ararat is numbered in the plate '4', and ends with Philadelphia of the Apocalypse numbered '66'. The Nile, which is sixth in sequence, is numbered '88'.

The commentary by the Revd Thomas Hartwell Horne BD is a typical Victorian text, a combination of learning and piety which assumes a good knowledge of the Bible in the readers. The underlying assumption is that belief in the essential truth of Holy Writ is reinforced by the reality of the landscape. There is a calm assurance that the version of events described in the Bible is the only true one. The dark shadow thrown by Darwinian evolution had not yet formed, although the troubled doubt of figures like the poet Tennyson was soon to appear. In the early part of the 19th century, the majority of people still visited the Holy Land as believers and therefore as a kind of pilgrim.

Travel to the Middle East had been made much simpler since the Napoleonic invasion of Egypt in 1798. Among the results of this disastrous adventure was the destabilisation of the power of the Mamluks, leading to their extinction by the new ruler, Mohammed Ali, who was more interested than they had been in ruthlessly modernising Egypt. Another consequence was a renewed, intense interest in the antiquities of Egypt and the Holy Land. Improvements in travel such as the development of steam boats and railways meant that visiting the holy places became quicker, cheaper and safer year by year.

Travel also had been encouraged by the necessity of improving communications with India, from which much of the wealth of Empire came. Great effort was spent in surveying and improving the routes to that essential colony. Any country that threatened Egypt, Syria or Turkey whose territory lay across the routes to India, menaced the lines of communication and supply. The great powers manoeuvred and threatened each other, but Turkish diplomacy successfully played off one contender against another, unlike Egypt which finally succumbed to British domination by the end of the century.

British travellers became more and more frequent in the region, something that John Murray and other publishers were not slow to exploit, providing travel guides as well as travel books in general for the increasing flow of tourists as the century progressed. Following this vogue for travel, a surge of illustrated books was published, but the first real anthology of views of the Holy Land was this our present book. It set a precedent for many other publications. Today the best known are by David Roberts, whose hand coloured lithographs were published in *The Holy Land, Syria, Idumea, Arabia, Egypt & Nubia* of 1842-9. He had travelled in 1838 to Egypt and Syria, inspired, it is said, by his work for the Findens.

FOREWORD

The Findens' romantic images are eagerly sought by collectors, and sadly, the volumes are often broken up and the pictures sold and framed individually. People treasure these delicate and painterly views, especially as they often represent a Middle East now changed utterly. The changes to the landscape are echoed in the changes in the landscape of religion. The images represented an untroubled assurance of faith, associated with a common belief, culture and education which are no longer to be taken for granted.

Charles Newton
27th May 1998

Prints & Drawings
Victoria & Albert Museum
London

INTRODUCTION.

WHILE other works of comparatively small value have employed the pencils of the first artists, and have received every sort of embellishment, little comparatively has been done towards illustrating the most important of all books — the HOLY SCRIPTURES. To supply this deficiency, is the design of the present collection of Landscape Illustrations, in which are exhibited nearly one hundred of the most remarkable places mentioned in the Bible, as they actually exist, and very few of which have hitherto been delineated. No expense has been spared in procuring, from the most eminent artists, drawings and engravings which should combine the utmost excellence of art, with the most exact and faithful adherence to the original sketches.

"If Troy and Thebes, if Athens and Rome, are visited with classic enthusiasm, how much more worthy of awakening the strongest emotions in the mind of a Christian must be the country whose history as far transcends in interest that of every other, as its literature (if we may apply that term to the divine volume) excels in sublimity all the ethics, and philosophy, and poetry, and eloquence of the heathen world."

Independently of the interesting associations connected with

> ———— " Those holy fields,
> Over whose acres walk'd those blessed feet,
> Which fourteen [eighteen] hundred years ago were nail'd,
> For our advantage, on the bitter cross," — (SHAKSPEARE.)

the Land of Palestine, as it is well known, abounds in scenes of the most picturesque beauty. Syria comprehends the snowy heights of Lebanon and the majestic ruins of Tadmor and Baalbec. The gigantic temples of Egypt, the desolate plains of Babylon and Nineveh, the ruined cities of Idumea, Moab, and Ammon, and the rocky solitudes of Mount Sinai,—all have afforded subjects most admirably adapted to the artist's pencil.

But it is not merely as a production exhibiting the highest improvements in the art of engraving, that this work is offered to the public. While the descriptions comprise the most accurate and authentic information which could be obtained concerning the scenes so graphically delineated in these volumes, the proprietors indulge the hope that these Landscape Illustrations of the Bible will be found eminently useful, as they comprise views, not only of the places where remarkable events actually took place, but also of those particularly mentioned in the prophecies, which in their present ruined and desolate condition exemplify, to the most minute particular, every thing that was foretold concerning them in the height of their prosperity. Egypt, Edom, Babylon, Nineveh, Tyre, Jerusalem, and the Apocalyptic Churches, may especially be adduced in illustration of this remark; so that in these instances the fulfilment of prophecy is actually set before the eye, while the understanding is assisted and confirmed by the sight.

A

GENERAL SKETCH

OF

THE HOLY LAND.

PALESTINE, the country inhabited for more than fifteen hundred years by the posterity of Jacob, was originally nothing more than the Greek name for the land of the Philistines; a tract of country situated on the coast of the Mediterranean Sea, and inhabited by the Philistines, who migrated from Egypt, and settled there after they had expelled the original inhabitants. This country is mentioned, both in sacred and in profane history, under various names, but at present it is most commonly known among all professors of the Christian name as the HOLY LAND: which appellation was first given to it by the prophet Zechariah (ii. 12.), as being the residence of God's peculiar people, the place where his sanctuary was established, and his presence visibly manifested. And this name has become still more applicable to the country, since it was the birth-place of the Redeemer, and the scene of his actions, discourses, and miracles.

It is difficult to fix the precise boundaries of the country inhabited by the Israelites, as its extent varied at different periods of the Jewish history, and as its limits are expressed in Scripture by reference to places, the exact situation of which is now uncertain. In general terms, however, it may be described as lying between the mountains of Lebanon on the north, the Mediterranean on the west, and the deserts of Arabia on the south. Beyond the

Jordan it stretched eastward, without any defined limit, into the region which lies between that river and the Euphrates. It was situated therefore between 31° and 33° 30′ north latitude, and between 34° 30′ and 37° east longitude from Greenwich. The exact dimensions, consequently, are uncertain. The whole length of the land is commonly denoted in the Old Testament by the phrase " from Dan to Beersheba," which places are supposed to have been about one hundred and fifty miles distant from each other. The greatest breadth, from east to west, probably did not exceed eighty miles.

Palestine is agreeably diversified with hill and dale: the Scriptures frequently mention it as a hilly country. (Exod. xv. 17. Deut. xi. 11. 1 Kings, xx. 23. Ezek. xxxiv. 13, 14.) Two parallel chains of mountains run from north to south, one on each side of the river Jordan, originating in the mountains of Lebanon, which divide Palestine from Syria, and terminating in the mountains of Horeb and Sinai, in Arabia Petræa. From these branch off a number of minor ridges, intersecting the whole country, and interrupted, here and there, by plains and spacious vallies. The whole region between Jaffa and Rama consists of a succession of gentle elevations and delightful fields and vallies.

In Judæa there are mountains of moderate height, uneven and irregular in shape. About and beyond Jericho, the hills are bare and barren, the vallies uncultivated, full of stones, and destitute of verdure. In the north, the mountains, though inferior in height, have a more inviting aspect, being covered with vegetation, and overlook fruitful vallies. The interior of the country is one great valley watered by the river Jordan, which flows from north to south, and empties itself into the Dead Sea. In the western part of the hill country the plains and vallies are numerous, and some of them extensive, but far less productive than the valley of the Jordan. The sea-coast, to which the name of Palestine more properly belongs, is almost entirely level, and not only without rivers, but even destitute of brooks, except such temporary rivulets as are produced by the melting of the snow in winter. Notwithstanding, the soil is black and rich, and, when the rains are regular, produces plentiful crops of grain and pulse.

Of the mountains above alluded to, the principal are Lebanon and Carmel (views of which will be found in the course of this work), Tabor, and the Mount of Olives. Among the rivers, the Jordan is pre-eminent; and of the minor streams, the brooks Kishon and Kedron are memorable in sacred history. They have furnished interesting subjects for the pencil.

Various are the expressions occurring in the Scriptures, in order to convey an idea of the fertility of the Holy Land. Thus, in Exod. iii. 8. xiii. 5. xxxiii. 3., and elsewhere, it is termed a "land flowing with milk and honey;" in Deut. iii. 25., a "good land;" in Neh. ix. 25. 35., a "fat land;" in Psalm cvi. 24. and Jer. iii. 19., "a pleasant land;" in Dan. xi. 6. 41., a "glorious land;" and in Exod. xx. 6., the "glory of all lands." The accounts of the sacred writers are fully confirmed by the testimonies of antient historians and modern travellers. Thus Tacitus says that "the natives are strong and patient of labour; the climate is dry and sultry; rain is seldom seen, and the soil is rich and fertile. Besides the fruits known in Italy, the palm and balm tree flourish in great luxuriance."* Justin confirms the account of Tacitus, respecting the abundant produce of the Holy Land, its beautiful climate, its palm and fragrant balsam trees.† The elder Pliny has celebrated the palms of Judæa‡; and the beauty of the country, as well as its large and handsome cities, are celebrated by Ammianus Marcellinus.§ The statements of these writers are fully corroborated by the Jewish historian Josephus, who has described his country as exuberant in fertility, richly cultivated and improved, and sustaining an immense population. ||

The statements of Maundrell, Dr. Shaw, Hasselquist, and other

---

* Taciti Hist., l. v. c. 26.
† Justin. Hist. Philippic., l. xxxvi. c. 3.
‡ Plinii Hist. Nat., l. xiii. c. 6.
§ Amm. Marcellin. Hist., l. xiv. c. 8.
|| Josephus de Bell. Jud., l. iii. c. 3. §§ 2—4. l. ii. c. 29. § 6.

modern travellers, abundantly confirm the attestations of antient writers. Not to multiply quotations unnecessarily,—Dr. E. D. Clarke thus describes the appearance of the country between Napolose or Sichem and Jerusalem:—" The road was mountainous, rocky, and full of loose stones; yet the cultivation was every where marvellous: it afforded one of the most striking pictures of human industry which it is possible to behold. The limestone rocks and vallies of Judæa were entirely covered with plantations of figs, vines, and olive trees; not a single spot seemed to be neglected. The hills, from their bases to their upmost summits, were entirely covered with gardens; all of these were free from weeds, and in the highest state of agricultural perfection. Even the sides of the most barren mountains had been rendered fertile by being divided into terraces, like steps rising one above another, whereon soil had been accumulated with astonishing labour. Under a wise and beneficent government, the produce of the Holy Land would exceed all calculation. Its perennial harvest; the salubrity of its air; its limpid springs; its rivers, lakes, and matchless plains; its hills and vales;—all these, added to the serenity of its climate, prove this land to be indeed ' a field which the Lord hath blessed' (Gen. xxvii. 27.): God hath given it of the dew of heaven, and the fatness of the earth, and plenty of corn and wine."*

" The whole of the country," says Mr. Buckingham, " on the east of the Jordan, from the Lake of Tiberias in the Dead Sea, and from Oomkais to Heshbon, is fertile in the extreme. The soil is so generally fertile, as to be capable of producing almost any thing that is required; and while the vallies abound with corn fields and olive grounds, the upland slopes of the hills are planted with vines, and the summits of the mountains are clothed with the trees of the coldest regions. The climate is really delightful; a clear, deep blue sky, a pure air, a warm summer in the vallies and plains, a snowy winter on the mountain tops, with all the finest shades of gradation between these two extremes, furnish

---

* Dr. Clarke's Travels, vol. ii. pp. 283—285.

every variety of temperature and atmosphere that can be desired by man." *

" Such being the state of the Holy Land, at least of that part of it which is properly cultivated, we can readily account for the vast population it antiently supported · and although this country, generally speaking, by no means corresponds with the statements we have of its former exuberant fertility and population, yet this is no contradiction to the narrative of the sacred writers. The devastations of the Holy Land by the Assyrians, Chaldees, Syrians, Romans, Saracens, the European Crusaders, and Turks, — together with the oppressions of the inhabitants by the Turks in our own times, — to which are to be added the depredations of robbers, and the predatory incursions of Arabs, — all concur satisfactorily to account for the present state of this country: and so far is it from contradicting the assertions of the sacred writings, that it confirms their authority: for, in the event of the Israelites proving unfaithful to their covenant engagements to Jehovah, all these judgments and predictions were denounced against them. (Lev. xxvi. 32. Deut. xxix. 22. et seq.) And the exact accomplishment of these prophecies affords a permanent comment on the declaration of the royal Psalmist, that a righteous God ' turneth a fruitful land into barrenness for the wickedness of them that dwell therein.' (Psalm cvii. 34.)" †

* Travels among the Arab Tribes, p. 121.
† Horne's Introduction to the Scriptures, vol. iii. p. 71.

CONTENTS

OF

THE FIRST VOLUME,

ARRANGED IN THE ORDER OF THE SEVERAL BOOKS OF SCRIPTURE.

	Title of the View.	By whom sketched.	By whom drawn.	* No. of Plate.
GEN. viii. 4.	Mount ARARAT - -	J. MORIER, Esq.	A. W. CALLCOTT.	4
x. 4.	KITTIM — Cyprus — Larnecea	M. CASSAS.	J. D. HARDING.	86
xxii.	Mount MORIAH -	Charles BARRY, Esq.	J. M. W. TURNER.	43
xxiii. 19.	HEBRON - -	Mrs. BRACEBRIDGE.	D. ROBERTS.	77
xxxvii. 12.	SHECHEM (Naplous), and MOUNT GERIZIM -	Capt. FITZMAURICE.	Capt. FITZMAURICE.	32
xli. 1.	EGYPT — The Nile, and Pyramids of Ghizeh -	F. CATHERWOOD, Esq.	C. STANFIELD.	88
EXOD. xxiv. 21.	The RED SEA, and Suez -	J. G. WILKINSON, Esq.	J. M. W. TURNER.	67
LEV. xxvii. 34.	Summit of MOUNT SINAI -	F. CATHERWOOD, Esq.	J. D. HARDING.	74
NUMB. i. 1.	MT. SINAI — Valley in which the Israelites encamped -	Gally KNIGHT, Esq.	J. M. W. TURNER.	7
DEUT. viii. 15.	WILDERNESS OF SINAI -	Major FELIX.	J. M. W. TURNER.	26
xxxiv. 3.	JERICHO - -	Sir A. EDMONSTONE.	J. M. W. TURNER.	47
JOSH. xi. 17.	Gate at Baalbec -	Charles BARRY, Esq.	C. STANFIELD.	62
xv. 5.	The DEAD SEA -	Rev. Robert MASTER.	J. M. W. TURNER.	10
xix. 29.	Ruins of TYRE -	J. BONOMI, Esq.	J. D. HARDING.	55
JUDG. iii. 28.	FORDS OF THE JORDAN - -	Rev. R. MASTER, and A. ALLEN, Esq.	A. W. CALLCOTT.	22
iv. 6.	Mount TABOR - -	Capt. FITZMAURICE.	J. D. HARDING.	41
v. 20.	River KISHON, and MT. CARMEL - - -	Capt. FITZMAURICE.	Capt. FITZMAURICE.	31
vi. 33.	The Plain of JEZREEL - -	Capt. FITZMAURICE.	Capt. FITZMAURICE.	81
1 SAM. xxiv. 1.	ENGEDI, and Convent of Santa Saba - -	Charles BARRY, Esq.	J. M. W. TURNER.	24
2 SAM. v. 6.	JERUSALEM — MOUNT ZION -	F. CATHERWOOD, Esq.	G. BULMER, Esq.	57
1 KINGS vi.	JERUSALEM—Mosque of Omar — Moriah - -	F. CATHERWOOD, Esq.	David ROBERTS.	75
ix. 18.	TADMOR in the DESERT -	C. R. WOOD, Esq.	C. STANFIELD.	6
xvi. 18.	SAMARIA - -	Mrs. BRACEBRIDGE and M. LÉON DE LABORDE.	David ROBERTS.	90
xviii. 19.	View from MOUNT CARMEL -	Rev. R. MASTER.	A. W. CALLCOTT.	17
2 KINGS ii. 19.	FOUNTAIN OF ELISHA -	Rev. R. MASTER.	A. W. CALLCOTT.	8
xiv. 7.	Ruins of SELAH (Petra) — Temple excavated out of the Rock - - -	M. LÉON DE LABORDE.	David ROBERTS.	33

* To assist the Binder in placing the Plates, they have been numbered with a small figure in the right hand corner, at the top.

	Title of the View.	By whom sketched.	By whom drawn.	No. of Plate.
2 Chron. ii. 16.	Joppa	Rev. R. Master.	J. M. W. Turner.	16
iii. 1.	Jerusalem — Pulpit in the Mosque of Omar	F. Catherwood, Esq.	S. Prout.	72
xxxii. 33.	Sepulchres of the Sons of David	M. De las Casas.	J. D. Harding.	64
Ps. lxxxix. 12.	Summit of Mount Tabor	Capt. Fitzmaurice.	Capt. Fitzmaurice.	94
Song of Sol. iv. 15.	View from Lebanon, down the Nahr el Kelb	Albert Way, Esq.	A. W. Callcott.	35
Eccles. ii. 4.	Solomon's Pools	Charles Barry, Esq.	J. M. W. Turner.	34
Isa. xix. 1.	Egypt—No-Amon—Thebes	F. Catherwood, Esq.	C. Stanfield.	73
xxxiii. 9.	The Cedars of Lebanon	Charles Barry, Esq.	J. D. Harding.	50
xxxviii. 24.	Lebanon, from Bairout	Capt. Fitzmaurice.	C. Stanfield.	27
lxvi. 19.	Egypt — Philæ	Charles Barry, Esq.	David Roberts.	28
Jer. xviii. 14.	Mount Lebanon, and Baalbec	Charles Barry, Esq.	A. W. Callcott.	3
xxxi. 15.	Ramah, and Rachel's Tomb	Rev. R. Master.	J. M. W. Turner.	49
xlvi. 25.	No-Amon — Portico at Karnak	Major Felix.	C. Stanfield.	30
xlix. 15.	Ruins of Petra. No. II.	M. Léon de Laborde.	David Roberts.	36
xlix. 17.	Edom — Entrance to Petra	Wm. J. Bankes, Esq.	J. D. Harding.	—
l. 38.	Babylon	Sir R. Ker Porter.	J. M. W. Turner.	21
Ezek. xxix. 10.	Temple of Isis in Ethiopia	Charles Barry, Esq.	A. W. Callcott.	20
xxxii.	Egypt, a near View of the Pyramids	Charles Barry, Esq.	J. M. W. Turner.	95
Hosea xiv. 5.	Mt. Lebanon, Convent of St. Antonio	Charles Barry, Esq.	J. M. W. Turner.	15
xiv. 7.	Distant View of the Cedars of Lebanon	Mrs. Bracebridge.	J. D. Harding.	84
Joel iii. 2.	Valley of Jehoshaphat,	Rev. R. Master.	David Roberts.	93
iii. 19.	Edom — Arch across the Ravine.	M. Léon de Laborde.	C. Stanfield.	57
Amos i. 4.	Damascus	Charles Barry, Esq.	A. W. Callcott.	46
Jonah i. 3.	Jaffa, the antient Joppa	Capt. Fitzmaurice.	Capt. Fitzmaurice.	89

Drawn by A.W Callcott R.A. from a sketch by James Morier Esq.

Engraved by E. Finden.

MOUNT ARARAT.

"AND THE ARK RESTED UPON THE MOUNTAINS OF ARARAT."

Gen. VIII. IV.

MOUNT ARARAT.

FROM THE HILLS ABOVE ERIVAN.

Drawn by A. W. CALLCOTT, from a Sketch made on the spot by J. MORIER, Esq.

And the ark rested . . . . upon the Mountains of Ararat.—Gen. viii. 4.

THIS celebrated mountain, on one of the ridges of which Noah's "ark rested in the seventh month, on the seventeenth day of the month," is situated in the greater Armenia; and, according to the calculation of Major Rennel, it lies in 39° 30′ north latitude, and 40° 30′ east longitude. By the Persians, in the neighbourhood, it is called *Kuhi-Nuach*, or the Mountain of Noah; and Turks, Armenians, and Persians, all unite in representing it as the haven of the great ship, which preserved the second father of mankind from the waters of the deluge. It consists of two peaks, which are called the Great and Little Ararat; and is twelve leagues distant from Erivan, rising majestically from a vast plain. The eternal snows upon its summits occasionally form avalanches, which precipitate themselves down its sides with a sound not unlike that of an earthquake. Various efforts have been made, at different times, by adventurous travellers, to scale these inaccessible mountain pyramids: all, however, were frustrated, except those of Professor Parrot, who, after various fruitless attempts, at length succeeded, in 1830, in overcoming every obstacle; and ascertained the positive elevation of the larger peak to be 16,200 French feet. It is, therefore, more than 1500 feet loftier than Mont Blanc. He describes the summit as being a circular plain about 160 feet in circumference, united by a gentle descent with a second and less elevated peak, lying towards the east. The whole of the upper region of the mountain, from the height of 12,750 English feet, is covered with perpetual snow and ice. Professor Parrot afterwards ascended the Little Ararat; which he reports to be about 13,100 English feet in height.

Our view is taken, looking towards the south. The edifice in the foreground is one of the numerous remains of churches and chapels scattered over the whole of Armenia. The figures represent one of the wandering tribes and their camels which are constantly passing southwards from the mountain districts to the plain, according to the season. The northern camels are highly esteemed as beasts of burthen, on account of their superior strength. *

* Sir R. K. Porter's Travels in Georgia, &c. vol. ii. pp. 182—184. Rennel's Geography of Herodotus, p. 239. Stuart's Hebrew Chrestomathy, p. 150. Andover Biblical Repository, vol. ii. p. 203. Cheek's Edinburgh Journal, No. 1. new series, Dec. 1830.

KITTIM, - CYPRUS.

View of Larnica.

GEN. X. 4.

Drawn by J. D. Harding from a sketch by Las Casas.

Engraved by W. Finden.

KITTIM — CYPRUS.

VIEW OF LARNECA.

Drawn by J. D. HARDING, from a View taken on the spot by M. CASSAS.

THE island of Cyprus was known to the Hebrews under the name of CHETIM (or Kittim), from Kittim the son of Javan, the son of Japhet, the son of Noah (Gen. x. 4.); who, according to the Jewish historian Josephus, in the division of territories, had the first possession of this island. Hence it followed that all islands and maritime places were called Chittim by the Hebrews. Josephus supports this opinion by shewing that Citium is a name corrupted from that of one of the cities of the island, which is derived from the appellation Chetim (or Kittim) borne by the whole island. He adds, that it was called Citius by those who use the language of the Greeks, and has not by the use of that dialect escaped the name of Cethium.*

Citium was one of the most antient cities in the island of Cyprus: it was founded by a Phœnician colony, and was celebrated as the birth-place of Zeno, the founder of the Stoic sect of philosophers, and also of the eminent Greek physician Apollonius, the disciple of Hippocrates. At the close of the Persian war, Citium was besieged and captured by the Athenian forces under Cimon, who died here in consequence of a wound which he had received during the siege. It is quite uncertain when this city was destroyed: the abbé Mariti believes that event did not take place later than the beginning of the third century. There is every reason to conclude that the antient city extended from the port all the way to the modern town of Larneca or Larnic, not only from the etymological meaning of its name (which signifies a *place of tombs*), but especially from the extensive sepulchral remains which occupy a considerable portion of the territory on which the modern town is situated.

Our view of Larneca is taken from the house of the Venetian consul.

---

* Jewish Antiquities, book i. ch. 7. (al. 6.)

Pt. 22.

The surrounding country is perfectly naked and rugged, and its climate is sultry and unwholesome. The consuls for the different European nations reside here, and their houses are fitted up in a handsome style. With the exception of some patches of verdure in what are called the gardens of some of the houses, the territory around is destitute of shade, and the ground is parched with heat.

*** Dr. Cramer's Geographical Description of Asia Minor, vol. ii. pp. 379, 380. Dr. Clarke's Travels, vol. iv. pp. 36—42. Carne's Letters from the East, p. 437.

43.

Drawn by J. M. W. Turner, R. A from a sketch by C. Barry, Esq.

Engraved by E. Finden.

MOUNT MORIAH.

2 CHRON. III. 1 GEN. XXII. 2.

MOUNT MORIAH.

Drawn by J. M. W. TURNER, from a Sketch made on the spot by CHARLES BARRY, Esq.

THE " Land of Moriah," mentioned in Gen. xxii. 2., is supposed to mean all the mountains, on which and on their hollows Jerusalem was afterwards erected, and these mountains were called " Moriah," or " Vision," because, being high land, they could be seen afar off; but afterwards the name was appropriated to the most elevated part, on which Solomon built his celebrated temple (2 Chron. iii. 1.), on the site of which now stands the mosque of Omar, which no Christian can enter but at the peril of his life. Dr. Richardson, however, whose skill and profession as a physician rendered him generally acceptable, obtained permission to explore this splendid monument of Saracenic magnificence, which forms a prominent object in our engraving.

MOUNT MORIAH, strictly so called, is the third of the four hills on which Jerusalem stood in the time of Jesus Christ, according to the minute topographical description of Josephus. This mountain is a rocky limestone hill, steep of ascent on every side except the north, and is surrounded on the other sides by a group of hills, in the form of an amphitheatre. (Psal. cxxv. 2.) On the east it borders the deep valley of Jehoshaphat, through which the Brook Kedron is seen flowing on the right. For a view of the Brook Kedron, see Part I.

*** Barbié du Bocage, Dictionnaire Géographique de la Bible, *voce* Moria. Josephus's History of the Jewish War, book v. ch. 4. Dr. Richardson's Travels, vol. ii. pp. 283—312.

77

HEBRON.

Mosque erected over the Graves of Abraham and the Patriarchs.

Drawn by D. Roberts from a sketch made on the spot, by Mrs Bracebridge.

Engraved by W. Finden.

GEN XXIII. 25. 1 CHRON III 12 13.

HEBRON.

TURKISH MOSQUE ERECTED OVER THE TOMBS OF ABRAHAM AND
THE PATRIARCHS.

Drawn by D. ROBERTS, from a Sketch made on the spot by Mrs. BRACEBRIDGE.

HEBRON is an antient city of Palestine, situated in the heart of the hill-country of Judæa, about twenty-seven miles south-west from Jerusalem. Originally, it was called Kirjath-Arba, or the city of Arba, " which Arba was a great man among the Anakims." (Josh. xiv. 15.) In the vicinity of this place Abraham abode, after he parted with Lot (Gen. xiii. 18.), and bought a field with a cave in which to bury his dead. (Gen. xxiii. 3—20.) Besides Abraham and Sarah, his son Isaac, his grandson Jacob, with their wives Rebekah and Leah, and his great-grandson Joseph, were severally interred here. (Gen. xxiii. 19. xxv. 10. xlix. 29—33. l. 12, 13.) When the Hebrews invaded Palestine, Hebron was the residence of a king (Josh. xii. 10.) named Hoham; who confederated with four other Canaanitish kings against Israel; but they were all discomfited and destroyed by Joshua. (Josh. x. 3, 4. 22—27.) After which the city, being taken, was assigned to Caleb (Josh. xiv. 6—11.) agreeably to a promise given him by Moses. (Numb. xiii. 30—33. xiv. 5. 24.) Subsequently, it was made a city of refuge, and given to the priests. (Josh. xxi. 11. xx. 7.) Afterwards, when David succeeded Saul on the throne of Israel, he selected Hebron for his royal residence, and continued there until Jerusalem was captured from the Jebusites. (2 Sam. ii. 1. v. 4—9. 1 Chron. xii. xiii.) On the division of the kingdom under Rehoboam, Hebron fell to the share of the king of Judah. (2 Chron. xi. 10.)

Hebron, Habroun, or, according to the Arabic orthography followed by the moderns, El Hhalil, is a flourishing town, the flat-roofed houses of which are closely jammed together. It contains about four hundred families of Arabs. The hill above it is composed of limestone rock, partially covered with vines; and its end is clothed with a wood of olives. The hill beyond the mosque, which edifice forms a prominent object in our view, and which has never before been delineated or engraved, is more barren; and in the fore-ground there are masses of buildings thrown down and scattered in every direction; this portion of the town having been destroyed a few years since. The inhabitants are engaged in perpetual hostilities with those of Bethlehem, on which account it is less frequently visited by pilgrims. A splendid church was erected over the graves of the patriarchs by the empress Helena: it has long been converted into a Turkish mosque. According to Ali Bey, who visited it in 1807, the ascent to it is by a large and fine staircase leading to a long gallery, the entrance to which is by a small court. Towards the left is a portico, resting upon square pillars. The vestibule of the temple contains two rooms; one of which is called the tomb of Abraham, the other that of Sarah. In the body of the church, between two large pillars on the right, is seen a small recess, in which is the sepulchre of Isaac, and in a similar one upon the left is that of his wife. On the opposite side of the court is another vestibule, which has also two rooms, respectively called the tombs of Jacob and his wife. At the extremity of the portico, on the right hand, is a door leading to a sort of long gallery, which still serves for a mosque; and passing from thence, is observed another room, said to contain the ashes of Joseph. All the sepulchres of the patriarchs are covered with rich carpets of green silk, magnificently embroidered with gold: those of their wives are red, embroidered in like manner. The sultans of Constantinople furnish these carpets, which are renewed from time to time. Ali Bey counted nine, one over the other, upon the sepulchre of Abraham. The rooms also which contain the tombs are covered with rich carpets: the entrance to them is guarded by iron gates, and wooden doors plated with silver, having bolts and padlocks of the same metal. More than a hundred persons are employed in the service of this Mohammedan temple. The population of Hebron is considerable: the inhabitants manufacture glass lamps, which are exported to Egypt. Provisions are abundant, and there is a considerable number of shops.

₊ Travels of Ali Bey, vol. ii. pp. 232, 233. Manuscript Communication from Mrs. Bracebridge.

PETRA.

"They shall build, but I will throw down."

MAL. 1. 4.

EDOM —(PETRA).

ENTRANCE TO PETRA.

Drawn by J. D. HARDING, from a Sketch made on the spot by WILLIAM JOHN BANKES, Esq.

IT was foretold by the prophet Jeremiah, that " Edom should be a desolation" (xlix. 17.) ; and the wild and desolate scenery delineated in our engraving sufficiently attests the fulfilment of this prediction. The present view represents the entrance to Petra by a hollow way, leading through magnificent ruins to the temple excavated out of this rock, which is exhibited and described in Part VI. : a glimpse of the temple appears in the distant back-ground. This way is a natural gorge or chasm between perpendicular rocks, and is lined with magnificent sepulchres.

As the very existence of the remarkable city of Petra or Selah may be considered as a recent discovery, and as all particulars respecting it are interesting, we will transfer to our pages the graphic description of Giovanni Finati, the guide who accompanied Mr. William Bankes, to whose valuable portfolio we are indebted for the sketch from which our view is taken.

" We rode on," he says, " winding till we found ourselves at last in the bottom, where the region of the tombs begins at the foot of the precipice.

" Like those of Egypt, they are all cut out in the live rock, but are yet the very opposite of them in one respect, for the decoration and extent are here all bestowed on the outside, and the interior is rude and diminutive, while in Egypt there is often externally no more than a simple doorway to be seen, though within there is chamber after chamber, all one more finished and ornamented than another, so that there can be no just point of comparison, unless, indeed, it should be to the great temples at Abousambul, to which these tombs seem inferior, if not in scale, at least in point of majesty of effect. Some have no more than a front, and some stand forward detached all round; the number altogether is prodigious, and the effect very strange, especially from the strong orange and purple tints of the sandstone itself. For a full mile there is no other passage excepting through a cleft, not more than three or four yards wide, of which the sides are sometimes perpendicular and sometimes overhanging, to the height of four or five hundred feet, which terrific pass

Pt. 19.

was the scene of a robbery and massacre the year before, in which a whole company of merchant-pilgrims returning from Mecca for Western Africa were the victims, some of whose goods were here and there offered us for sale in our return, but who were the actual perpetrators seemed to be uncertain.

"About half way through, there is a single spot, abrupt and precipitous as the rest, where the area of this natural chasm spreads a little, and sweeps into an irregular circle; this was chosen for the situation of the most elaborate, if not the most extensive of all the architectural monuments, which, from a large vase (furnished as it should seem originally with handles of metal) placed upon its summit, and supposed by the natives to be filled with coin, is called the treasure-house of Pharaoh. Bullets seem to have been fired at the vase in great numbers, but quite without effect, and it stands at such a height, and in such a position, that perhaps even avarice and curiosity have never succeeded in climbing to it, being as inaccessible from above, by the rude overhanging of the rock, as from below by the smoothness of the wrought surface; for, with columns, and rich friezes, and pediments, and large figures of horses and men, the front rises to several lofty stories, and the surprising effect is heightened by the position, and the strangeness of the approach. The detail is so minute and so well preserved, that Mr. Bankes's drawing of this front alone was the work of many hours, the rest waiting patiently in the mean time in a tuft of oleanders that grows before it.

"Immediately beyond, the ravine closes and contracts again to its former limits, and expands no more till it opens at once on the ruins of the city, which may rather be said to stand in a hollow of a mountain than either in a valley or a plain. A small stream that ran through it was arched over; one large pile of masonry is standing, and here and there a few columns, but all the rest was excavation; for there were houses gained out of the rocks, as well as a theatre, and an immense display of tombs all round, which (if indeed some might not be temples) form the most striking object even from the very centre of the old city, many rising to a vast height, like our Italian churches, with ranges of pillars and ornaments one above the other, but the majority restricted to a much simpler form, peculiar to the place, terminating with flights of steps on the top as a battlement."

₊ The Life and Adventures of Giovanni Finati, vol. ii. pp. 261—265.

Drawn by the Hon. W. E. Fitzmaurice, from a sketch taken by him on the spot, 1833.　　　　　　　Engraved by E. Finden.

THE TOWN OF SHECHEM, (NAPLOUS.)

Under Mount Gerizim. Looking South.

GEN.XXXVII.12,14.-JOSH.VIII.33.-JOHN IV. 5.

THE TOWN OF SCHECHEM, or SYCHAR (Naplous),

under Mount Gerizim, looking south.

Drawn by the Hon. Capt. Fitzmaurice, from a Sketch made on the spot by Himself.

Shechem, Sichem, or Sychar, as it is variously called in the Scriptures, was one of the oldest cities in Palestine. It was a city in Jacob's time (Gen. xxxiii. 18.), if not in the time of Abraham. (Gen. xii. 6.) When Jacob returned from Mesopotamia, it was in the possession of Hamor, a Hivite prince. (Gen. xxxiii. 19. xxxiv. 2.) On the division of the land among the tribes, this city fell to Ephraim (Josh. xxi. 21.), but it was appropriated to the Levites. Here Joshua assembled the people before his death, and renewed the covenant between them and Jehovah. (Josh. xxiv.) After the death of Gideon, Shechem became a seat of idolatrous worship, the people worshipping Baal-berith there. (Judg. viii. 33. ix. 4. 46.) The people of Shechem resisted the usurpation of Abimelech, who therefore brought an army against it, and " took the city, and slew the people that was therein, and beat down the city, and sowed it with salt." (Judg. ix. 45.) Subsequently, however, it was rebuilt, for it is mentioned by David in Psalm lx. 6. Hither, on the death of Solomon, all Israel came to make Rehoboam king (1 Kings xii. 1.), and, on his non-compliance with their demands, ten tribes elected Jeroboam I. for their sovereign, who chose Shechem for his residence, and built [that is, rebuilt] and adorned it (25.).

On the return of the Jews from the Babylonish captivity, the mixed race who inhabited Samaria were desirous of assisting in the erection, and of participating in the privileges, of the temple at Jerusalem, but were refused. They therefore built a temple for themselves, on Mount Gerizim, where, under the direction of Manasseh, a Jewish priest, they worshipped in strict observance of the law of Moses. This temple stood two hundred years, and was finally destroyed B. c. 129. In John iv. 5. Shechem is called Sychar: by the Romans it was called Flavia Neapolis, in honour of the emperor Flavius Vespasian : its modern appellation is Napolose, which the Arabs have corrupted into Nablous, or Naplous.

Napolose, or Sichem, is romantically situated in a deep valley, between the mountains of Ebal on the left, and Gerizim on the right : our view (which has never before been engraved) is taken, looking from Gerizim

Pt. 11.

towards Ebal. There is a kind of sublime horror in the lofty, craggy, and barren aspect of these two mountains, which seem to face each other with an air of defiance; especially as they stand contrasted with the rich valley beneath, where the city appears to be embedded on either side in green gardens and extensive olive-grounds, rendered more verdant by the lengthened period of shade which they enjoy from the mountains on each side. Along the valley, in which Sichem stands, Dr. Clarke beheld " a company of Ishmaelites coming from Gilead," as in the days of Reuben and Judah, " with their camels bearing spices, and balm and myrrh," who would gladly have purchased another Joseph of his brethren, and conveyed him as a slave to some Potiphar in Egypt. (Gen. xxxvii. 25. 36.) Upon the surrounding hills flocks and herds were feeding as of old (13.), nor in the simple garb of the shepherds was there any thing to contradict the notions we may entertain of the appearance formerly exhibited by the sons of Jacob.

In the vicinity of Sichem travellers are still directed to the sepulchres, in which the remains of Joseph, of Eleazar the high priest, and of Joshua, are said to have been severally deposited. (Josh. xxiv. 29, 30. 32, 33.) But the principal object of veneration, among the inhabitants, is JACOB's WELL (John iv. 56.); so called, because it was " near to the parcel of ground that Jacob gave to his son Joseph." (John iv. 3. Gen. xlviii. 22.)

There is nothing finer in the Holy Land than the view of Naplous from the eminences which surround it: it is, indeed, considered as the finest city in Syria; but all its beauty is lost upon an European from the narrowness of the streets. There is, however, a very fine bazaar; and to a stranger nothing is more striking than these Eastern markets. The building is generally of an oblong form; here it was about two hundred yards long: in the centre is a footway for the foot passengers and camels; and on each side are broad counters, where the Jews and Turks sit cross-legged, smoking their pipes and drinking coffee, and offering their goods for sale. Trade appears to flourish among the inhabitants of this city: their principal employment is in making soap; but the manufactures of the town supply a very extended neighbourhood, and they are carried to a great distance upon camels.

₊ Dr. Clarke's Travels in Greece, &c. vol. iv. pp. 267—280. Alexander's Geography of the Bible, p. 135. (Philadelphia, 1830.) Jowett's Christian Researches in Syria, p. 193. The Hon. Capt. Fitzmaurice's (unpublished) Cruise to Egypt, Palestine, and Greece, p. 53.

E G Y P T.

The river NILE, with the Pyramids.

Drawn by C. Stanfield, R.A. from a sketch taken on the spot by T. Catherwood.

Engraved by W. Finden.

CH. XLI. 1.

1 KON. L. 22. II. 3. 5.

EGYPT.

THE RIVER NILE,

WITH THE PYRAMIDS OF GHIZEH IN THE DISTANCE.

Drawn by C. STANFIELD, from a Sketch made on the spot by F. CATHERWOOD, Esq.

THE NILE is the only river of Egypt, and is called by way of pre-eminence THE RIVER, in Gen. xli. 1. and Exod. i. 22. Some critics have supposed it to be the Sihor or Shihor mentioned in Isa. xxiii. 3. and 1 Chron. xiii. 5. This river takes the name of THE NILE only after the junction of the two great streams of which it is composed, viz. The *Bahr el Abiad* or White River, which rises near the equator, in the Mountains of the Moon, in the interior of Africa, and runs northward till it is joined by the other branch, the *Bahr el Azrek* or Blue River, which rises in Abyssinia; and, after a large circuit to the south-east and south-west, in the course of which it passes through the lake of Dembea, it flows northward to join the White River. This Abyssinian branch has, in modern times, been regarded as the real Nile, although the White River is by far the largest and longest, and was antiently considered as the true Nile. The junction takes place about lat. 16 north. From this point the river flows in a northerly direction, with the exception of one large bend to the west. It receives the Tacazze, a large stream from Abyssinia, and, after passing through Nubia, it enters Egypt at the cataracts near Syene or Essouan; which are formed by a chain of rocks stretching east and west. There are three falls, after which the river pursues its course, in still and silent majesty, through the whole length of Egypt. In Lower Egypt it divides into several branches, about forty or fifty miles from the sea-coast, which form with the latter a triangle, the base of which is the sea-coast: and having thus the shape of the Greek letter *delta* (Δ), this part of Egypt antiently received the name of the Delta, which it has retained ever since.

The whole physical and political existence of Egypt may be said to depend on the Nile; for in this country, where rain is almost unknown, without the Nile, and also without its regular annual inundations, the whole land would be a desert. Its water, after being filtered, is acknowledged by all travellers, antient and modern, to be peculiarly sweet and even delicious; hence we may form some idea of the nature of that afflictive judgment, by which the waters were turned into blood (Exod. vii. 17—21.).

The inundations of the Nile are caused by regular periodical rains in the countries farther south, around the sources of the river, in March and later. The river begins to rise in Egypt about the middle of June, and continues to increase through the month of July. In August it overflows its banks, and reaches the highest point early in September. The whole land is then generally under water. In the beginning of October the inundation still continues; and it is only towards the end of this month that the stream returns within its banks. From the middle of August till towards the end of October, the whole land of Egypt resembles a vast lake or sea, in which the towns and cities appear as islands. This inundation appears to be referred to, in Amos, viii. 8. and ix. 5. The fertility, which the Nile thus imparts to the soil, is caused not only by its irrigation of the land, but also by the thick slimy mud, which its waters bring down with them and deposit thereon. It is like a coat of rich manure; and the seed being sown immediately upon it, without digging or ploughing, springs up rapidly, grows with luxuriance, and ripens into abundance. By means of canals and trenches, the whole adjacent regions receive the benefit of these floods; and, in order to raise the water to the high grounds, machines have been used in Egypt from time immemorial. These are chiefly wheels to which baskets are attached: one kind is turned by oxen; and another smaller sort, by men treading upon them; to this last mode of raising water there appears to be an allusion in Deut. xi. 10. The history of Egypt abounds with records of distress and famine, caused by the failure of this inundation; and the prophets denounced this calamity as a punishment upon the Egyptians. (Isa. xix. 5, 6. Ezek. xxx. 12.)

As the inundations of the Nile are of so much importance to the whole land, columns have ever been erected, on which the beginning and progress of its rise might be observed. These are called *Nilometers*, that is, Measurers of the Nile. At present there is one on the little island of Roda, opposite to Cairo, which is under the care of the government: it consists of a square well or chamber, in the centre of which is a graduated pillar for the purpose of ascertaining the daily rise of the Nile. This is proclaimed every morning in the streets of the capital by four criers, to each of whom a portion of the city is assigned.

If the inundation reaches the height of twenty-two feet, a rich harvest is expected, because then all the fields have received the requisite irrigation. If it falls short of

THE RIVER NILE.

this height, and in proportion as it thus falls short, the land is threatened with want and famine, of which many horrible examples occur in Egyptian history: should the rise of the water exceed twenty-eight feet, a famine is in like manner feared.

The opening of the canal, which carries the water to Cairo, generally takes place during the first fortnight in August; and, the night previous, festivities of all kinds commence on the river in front of its mouth, and are continued until daybreak. The signal for cutting the dam is given by the kiaia or deputy of the pasha; and money is sparingly thrown into its bed, and eagerly scrambled for by the peasants (sometimes with loss of life by drowning) in the falling stream of the canal.

The Hebrews sometimes give the appellation of sea to the Nile as well as to the river Euphrates (Isa. xix. 5. Nahum, iii. 8.): in this they are borne out by the Arabic writers, who speak of the Nile as a sea. The Nile is also to the present day celebrated for its fish. (Compare Numb. xi. 5. and Isa. xix. 8.) In its waters are found the crocodile or leviathan, and the hippopotamus or behemoth.

The Pyramids, which are seen in the back ground of our engraving, are those of Géezeh, Ghizeh, or Djizeh (as the name is variously written), a village about ten miles distant from Cairo, when the Nile is low; but, when the inundation is at its height, a very circuitous route becomes necessary, and the distance is not less than twenty miles. The two largest are nearly of equal height, but the third is considerably smaller. These extraordinary structures, which are little short of three thousand years old, and which promise to last until the end of time, are supposed to have combined the twofold object of a sepulchre and an observatory. On a first view of them, the traveller feels much disappointed: as they stand in the midst of a flat and boundless desert, and as there is no elevation near, with which to contrast them, it is not easy to form a conception of their real magnitude, until, after repeated visits and observations, their vast size fills the mind with astonishment.

The largest of these pyramids, which on the authority of Herodotus is ascribed to Cheops, covered an area of about 570,000 square feet: but now that it has been stript of its exterior tier of stones, the total length of each face, without the casing, is reduced to 732 feet, and its actual height to 474. The entrance is nearly in the centre; and a passage, descending at an angle of twenty-seven degrees, terminates in an unfinished chamber below the level of the ground. About a hundred feet from the entrance, this passage is joined by an upper one, which ascends at the same gallery, when it runs horizontally into what is called the Queen's chamber: but the gallery itself, continuing at an angle of twenty-seven degrees, leads to a larger room called the King's chamber, in which is a sarcophagus of red granite. At the bottom of the gallery itself is the well, by which the workmen descended, after they had closed the lower end of the upper passage with blocks of granite. This pyramid is said to have been opened by the sultan Mamoun, about the year 820. Mr. Wilkinson is of opinion that several chambers still exist, though undiscovered, in the upper part of this pyramid.

The style of building in the second pyramid, which bears the name of Cephren, or Cephrenes, king of Egypt, is inferior to that of the first; the stones, used in its construction, being less carefully selected, though united with nearly the same kind of cement. Nor (says Mr. Wilkinson) was all the stone of either pyramid brought from the quarries of the Arabian mountains, but the outer tier or casing was composed of blocks hewn from their compact strata. This casing, part of which still remains on the pyramid of Cephrenes, is in fact merely formed by levelling or planing down the upper angle of the projecting steps, and was consequently commenced from the summit. The passages in this pyramid are very similar to those of the first, but there is no gallery; and they lead only to one main chamber, in which is a sarcophagus sunk in the floor. This pyramid appears to have had two entrances; an upper one by which the visitor now enters, and another about sixty feet below it, which is still unopened. The actual height of this pyramid is about 439 feet; and the length of its base, 690; but if it were entire, its height would be increased to about 469 feet. This pyramid was explored by the enterprising traveller Belzoni, to whose work the reader is necessarily referred for an account of his very interesting researches.

The third pyramid, which in our engraving blends in with the back ground, bears the name of Mycerinus, Moscheris, or Mecherinus. It has not yet been opened; and it differs from the other two, being built in almost perpendicular degrees, to which a sloping face has been afterwards added. The outer layers (many of which still remain) were of red granite, of which material the exterior of the lowest row of the second pyramid was also composed, as is evident by the blocks and fragments which lie scattered about its base.

₊ Carne's Letters from the East, pp. 102—106. Dr. Clarke's Travels, vol. v. pp. 171—199. Dr. Richardson's Travels, vol. i. pp. 117—144. Belzoni's Travels, vol. i. pp. 397—407. 8vo edit. Robinson's Dictionary of the Bible, voce Nile (Boston, Massachussetts, 1831). Mr. Wilkinson's Topography of Thebes, &c. pp. 311—330. A very interesting account of the excavations of M. Caviglia among the pyramids is given in the Quarterly Review, vol. xix. pp. 397. et seq.

Drawn by J. M. W. Turner, R. A. from a sketch taken on the spot by J. C. Wilkinson, Esq.

Engraved by E. Finden.

THE RED SEA.

At Suez.

EXODUS XIV. 21 PSALMS LXXVIII. 13 CVI. 7

THE RED SEA, AND THE PORT OF SUEZ.

Drawn by J. M. W. Turner, from a Sketch by J. G. Wilkinson, Esq.

" He rebuked the Red Sea also, and it was dried up." Psalm cvi. 9.
Exodus, xiv. 21.

The Red Sea separates Egypt from Arabia. The name, in Hebrew, signifies the " Weedy Sea," or the " Sea of Weeds," which appellation it still retains in the Coptic language. It is thus denominated, according to some authors, from the variety of sea-weeds which are said to be visible at low water; but Mr. Bruce, who had examined its whole extent, states that he never observed a single weed in it. He further remarks, that a narrow gulf, under the immediate influence of monsoons blowing from contrary points during six months in each year, would be too much agitated to produce such vegetables, which are seldom found but in stagnant waters, and still more rarely — if ever — found in salt waters. He is of opinion that this sea takes its name from the large trees or plants of white coral, which bear a perfect resemblance to plants on land. We derive the name " Red Sea" from the Greeks. Most probably this sea was antiently called the " Sea of Edom," from the neighbouring coast; and as Edom signifies *red* in Hebrew, the Greeks, not understanding the meaning of the appellation, translated it (as we have done after them) the Red Sea.

This sea is memorable for the miraculous passage over it by the Israelites on their departure from Egypt. They broke up from Rameses in the land of Goshen about the middle of April, and journeyed south- wards below Suez; when, by means of a strong north-east wind, the Almighty drove out the waters of the sea in such a way, that the Israelites passed over the bed of it on dry ground, while the Egyptians who at- tempted to follow them were drowned by the returning waters. Various antient traditions among the heathen historians attest the reality of the miraculous passage of the Red Sea by the Israelites; to which we may add, that it is manifest from the text of Moses and of other sacred authors, who have mentioned this miraculous passage, that no other account can be supported, but that which supposes the Hebrews to cross the sea from shore to shore, in a vast space of dry ground, which was left void by the waters at their retiring. (Exod. xiv.) To omit the numerous allusions in the book of Psalms, Isaiah says, God divided the waves before his people, and that he conducted them through the bottom of the abyss, as a horse is led through the midst of a field. (Isa. lxiii. 11, &c.) Habakkuk (iii. 15.) says, that the LORD made himself a road, to drive his chariot and horses across the sea, through the heap of great waters. Lastly, in the apocryphal book of Wisdom (xix. 7, 8. x. 17, 18.) we read, that the dry land appeared all on a sudden, in a place where water stood before; that a free passage was opened in a moment through the midst of the Red Sea; and that a green field was seen in the midst of the deep.

The PORT OF SUEZ stands at the mouth of the canal which formerly united the Red Sea with the Mediterranean, (marked, on the left of our engraving, by a line of stones in the water, which probably are the remains of antient piers or masonry,) and upon the northern point of the Red Sea, on a tongue of land, which some commentators have supposed to be " the tongue of the Egyptian Sea" mentioned in Isa. xi. 15., in which place there is an evident allusion to the miraculous passage of the Israelites. The sea runs up nearly to the low wall surrounding the town, which is seen on the right of the same engraving: it is tolerable even as a Turkish town; and, were it in other hands, it would be delightful. There is a large square, and there is an attempt at regularity of building; and its situation is described as being beautiful. The old walls of Suez, and the remains which are still left of its harbour, are constructed of fossil shells, testimonies of the deluge. " The Red Sea is about fifteen hundred miles from one extremity to the other: it is visited by a few European vessels, which trade principally to Mocha. The pasha of Egypt maintains a small fleet upon it, for the passage and protection of his troops; and the vessels of the bordering countries are seen skimming along in all directions, laden deep with passengers. The coasts are lined with coral, sometimes of a most beautiful construction; and when the day is calm, or the night is dark and still, the mariner might think himself transported to some enchanted land, the water is so clear, the coruscations of light are so radiant, and the coral beneath so extensively ramified. But the coasting vessels are often, from the same cause, in extreme danger; and though they are furnished with a false keel, this is not always proof against the violent shocks they have to bear."

The vessel represented in the foreground of our engraving is of the kind peculiar to the Red Sea, called a *Dao;* and is, perhaps, of the same shape and fashion as those which were launched by Solomon at " Ezion-geber, which is beside Eloth, on the shore of the Red Sea" (2 Kings, ix. 26.), and afterwards by Jehoshaphat, to trade with Ophir, whose vessels, however, were wrecked at Ezion-geber. (2 Kings, xxii. 48.) The materials of these ships were transported overland from Gaza, having been originally brought from Mount Lebanon. This is a common occurrence at the present day on the shores of the Red Sea, where no tree grows. M. Laborde mentions that scarcely a year elapses in which the timbers of vessels may not be seen passing, in single pieces, through the streets of Suez, on their way to the shore, in order to be put together and launched.

₊ Dr. Shaw's Travels, vol. ii. pp. 92—104. 329. Carne's Letters, p. 175. Bruce's Travels, vol. ii. p. 188. Horne's Introduction to the Scriptures, vol. iii. pp. 612, 613. Sir Frederick Henniker's Notes during a Visit to Egypt, &c. pp. 216, 217. Hardy's Notices of the Holy Land, pp. 20, 21.

Drawn by J. D. Harding, from a sketch by F. Catherwood.

THE SUMMIT OF SINAI.

LEVIT. XXVII. 34.

Engraved by E. Finden.

THE SUMMIT OF MOUNT SINAI.

Drawn by J. D. Harding, from a Sketch made on the spot by F. Catherwood, Esq.

The general features of Mount Sinai having already been described in Parts V. and XI. of this Work, but little remains to be added in illustration of the view which is now submitted to the reader: it represents the summits of this stupendous mountainous range, where the Almighty is believed to have given "the commandments, which the Lord commanded Moses for the children of Israel." (Levit. xxvii. 34.) There is, however, considerable difficulty in determining the particular spot honoured by the Deity for the promulgation of his will to his chosen people. The three highest summits in the Arabian peninsula are Mounts Saint Catherine, Serbal, and Shomar; and to each of them has been attributed the distinction of having witnessed the promulgation of the decalogue. Our view exhibits what is currently regarded as the summit of Mount Sinai: it is the nearest summit to the convent of Mount Saint Catherine, and is about an hour's fatiguing ascent. A flight of steps (now ruined, but plainly discernible) leads from a spot near the convent quite to the top: these granite steps are taken from the sides of the mountain, and are at least as antient as the foundation of the convent, or perhaps even much earlier. This at least proves that, for many centuries, the spot whence our view is taken, has been considered as the actual summit of this mountain, or Horeb. The prospect which it commands is very extensive and grand, but at the same time of the most desolate description. As far as the eye can reach, nothing is to be seen on every side but vast ranges of naked mountains succeeding each other like waves of the sea. Between these rocky chains there are in general only ravines or narrow vallies. Mohammedans, Christians, and Jews equally hold Mount Sinai in the profoundest respect.

The ruined building which is seen in our engraving represents the ruins of a Turkish mosque; and not far from it are the remains of a Greek chapel, in the immediate vicinity of which there is a well of excellent water. In the time of Frescobaldi (1384) this chapel was

Pt. 19.

adorned with paintings and closed with an iron door. When visited by Belon in 1550, and subsequently by Pölschitz in 1598, its gate or door was still standing : but already had the pilgrims to the Holy Land covered its walls with their names and with common-place reflections. In 1610 Sandys found the whole a ruin.

₊ Manuscript Communication from F. Catherwood, Esq. Léon de Laborde, Voyage de l'Arabie Petrée, p. 68. An accurate English translation of M. Laborde's splendid but costly sketches of his journey through Arabia Petrée to MOUNT SINAI and the excavated city of Petra (with the plates carefully re-engraved) has been published by Mr. Murray (the publisher of this work), in a form and at a price which render it easily accessible to the majority of readers.

7

Drawn by J. M. W Turner R.A from a sketch by Gally Knight Esqʳ

Engraved by James B. Allen.

THE VALLEY IN WHICH THE CHILDREN OF ISRAEL WERE ENCAMPED.

Mount Sinai in the Distance.

NUMBERS 1. 1

MOUNT SINAI.

The Valley in which the Children of Israel are supposed to have encamped.

Drawn by J. M. W. Turner, from a Sketch made on the spot by Gally Knight, Esq.

The upper region of the mountainous range, in the peninsula of Arabia, which is collectively termed Sinai, forms an irregular circle of thirty or forty miles in diameter; it possesses numerous sources of water, a temperate climate, and a soil capable of supporting animal and vegetable nature. This, therefore, was the part of the peninsula best adapted to the residence of nearly a year, during which the Israelites were numbered, and received their laws from the Most High. This tract is thus described by Mr. Burckhardt, who visited it in the spring of 1816:—" The upper nucleus of Sinai, composed almost entirely of granite, forms a rocky wilderness of an irregular circular shape, intersected by many narrow valleys, and from thirty to forty miles in diameter. It contains the highest mountains of the peninsula, whose shaggy and pointed peaks, and steep and shattered sides, render it clearly distinguishable from all the rest of the country in view. It is upon the highest region of the peninsula, that the fertile valleys are found, which produce fruit trees: they are principally to the west and south-west of the convent [of Mount Sinai], at three or four hours distant. Water, too, is always found in plenty in this district; on which account it is the place of refuge of all the Bedouins, when the low country is parched up." He therefore thinks that this upper country, or " wilderness," is exclusively the *Desert of Sinai*, so often mentioned in the account of the wanderings of the Israelites (compare Numb. i. 1. and xxxiii. 15. with Exod. xix. 1, &c.) In approaching the elevated region from the north-west, Burckhardt writes: — " We now approached the central summits of Mount Sinai, which we had in view for several days. Abrupt cliffs of granite, from six to eight hundred feet in height, whose surface is blackened by the sun, surround the avenues leading to the elevated region to which the name of Sinai is specifically applied. These cliffs inclose the holy mountain on three sides. At the end of three hours we entered these cliffs by a narrow defile about forty feet in breadth, with perpendicular granite rocks on

Pt. 11.

both sides. The ground is covered with sand and pebbles, brought down by the torrent which rushes from the upper region in the winter time." To the opinion of this very intelligent and judicious traveller we may well yield our assent, especially as it was formed from personal observation made on the spot with great patience and accuracy. In this wilderness the Israelites remained during all the transactions recorded in Exod. xix. to the end, in Leviticus, and in the first nine chapters of the book of Numbers. In Num. x. 11. it is recorded, that " on the twentieth day of the second month, in the second year, the cloud was taken up, and the children of Israel took their journey out of the wilderness of Sinai." Their sojourn at Sinai may therefore be counted from the fifteenth day of June to the twentieth of May following ; a period of eleven months and five days, according to our mode of reckoning : but, as they reckoned by lunar months, the whole interval was, in fact, something less than eleven of our months.

₊ Burckhardt's Travels in Syria, &c. pp. 673, &c. Biblical Repository (Andover, Massachusetts), vol. ii. p. 771.

THE DESERT OF SINAI.

With the Rock said by the Arabs to be that which Moses struck.

"That great and terrible Wilderness"

DEUT. VIII 16.

Drawn by J.M.W.Turner, R.A. from a sketch by Major Felix.

Engraved by E.Finden.

THE WILDERNESS OF SINAI.

Drawn by J. M. W. Turner, from a Drawing made on the spot by Major Felix.

" That great and terrible wilderness, where *there was* no water." Deut. viii. 15.

Sinai is a mountainous range of Arabia Petræa, in the Peninsula formed by the two northern arms of the Red Sea: it is rendered memorable as the place where the law was given to the Israelites by Moses (Exod. xix. xx.), and it comprehends many peaks, which are almost entirely composed of granite, forming a rocky wilderness, of an irregular circular shape, intersected by many narrow vallies, and from thirty to forty miles in diameter. It has two principal elevations, by the Arabs called *Gebel Mousa*, or the Mountain of Moses, and *Gebel Katerin*, or the Mountain of St. Catherine, which are generally identified with Sinai and Horeb, though little dependence is to be placed upon local tradition.

Mount Sinai, strictly so called, is a long narrow hill, to the west and south-west of which lies a narrow valley, which Dr. Pococke terms the Vale of Jah, or the Vale of God: this he considers to be the vale or plain of Rephidim, where the Israelites encamped when they came out of the Desert of Sin. Here is shown the rock exhibited in our engraving, which Moses is traditionally said to have struck, when the waters miraculously gushed forth, and supplied the thirsty and fainting Israelites. (Exod. xvii. 1—7. Numb. xx. 7—11.) From its hardness, it is appropriately termed a " rock of flint," in Deut. viii. 15. Dr. Shaw states it to be about six yards square: but Dr. Pococke (with whose calculations Mr. Carne very nearly agrees) says that it is a beautiful red granite stone, about fifteen feet long, ten feet wide, and about twelve feet high. It lies, tottering and loose, near the middle of the valley, which is here about two hundred yards broad; and it seems to have been formerly a part or cliff of Mount Sinai, which hangs in a variety of precipices over all this plain.

There are four or five fissures, one above the other, on the face of the rock, and each of them is about a foot and a half long, and a few inches deep. What is very remarkable, they run along the breadth of the rock, and are not rent downwards: they are more than a foot asunder, and there is a channel worn between them by the gushing of the waters. To the miraculous supply of the perishing Israelites, the Psalmist thus

Pt. 5.

alludes:—" He clave the rocks in the wilderness, and gave them drink as *out of* the great depths. He brought streams also out of the rock, and caused waters to run down like rivers." (Psal. lxxviii. 15, 16.) " He opened the rock and the waters gushed out: they ran in the dry places like a river." (Psal. cvii. 41.)

Neither art nor chance, Dr. Shaw remarks, could be concerned in the contrivance, inasmuch as every circumstance points out to us a miracle: and it never fails to produce the greatest seriousness and attention in all who behold it. That learned and accurate traveller was in danger of being stoned by his Arab guards for attempting to break off a corner of it. The Arabs call this rock of Meribah the Stone of Moses: it is greatly venerated by the Bedouins who put grass into the fissures above described, as offerings to the memory of Moses, in the same manner as they place grass upon the tombs of their saints, because grass is to them the most precious gift of nature, and that upon which their existence chiefly depends. They also bring hither their female camels: for they believe that, by making the animal couch down before the rock, while they recite some prayers, and by putting fresh grass into the fissures of the stone, the camels will become fruitful, and yield an abundance of milk. This superstition is encouraged by the monks, who rejoice to see the Mohammedan Bedouins venerating the same object with themselves. When Mr. Carne visited this spot, a few years since, two of the holes were filled with reeds for this purpose.

⁎ Pococke's Description of the East, vol. i. pp. 143, 144. Shaw's Travels, vol. i. pp. 108—110. Burckhardt's Tour in Syria, &c. pp. 578—580. Carne's Letters, pp. 198, 199.

Drawn by J. M. W. Turner, R. A. from a sketch by the Revd R. Master.

Engraved by W Finden.

JERICHO.

JOSHUA VI.

JERICHO.

Drawn by J. M. W. Turner, from a Sketch made on the spot by Sir A. Edmondstone.

Jericho, " the city of palm trees" (Deut. xxxiv. 3.), derives all its importance from history. Though now only a miserable village, containing about thirty wretched cottages, which are inhabited by half-naked Arabs, it was one of the oldest cities in Palestine, and was the first place reduced by the Israelites on entering the Holy Land. It was rased to the ground by Joshua, who denounced a curse on the person who should rebuild it. (Josh. vi. 20. 26.) Five hundred and thirty years afterwards this malediction was literally fulfilled upon Hiel of Bethel (1 Kings xvi. 34.), who rebuilt the city, which soon appears to have attained a considerable degree of importance. There was a school of the prophets here in the days of Elijah and Elisha, both of whom seem to have resided much here. In the vicinity of Jericho there was a large but unwholesome spring, which rendered the soil unfruitful, until it was cured by the prophet Elisha. (2 Kings, ii. 21.) Of this spring or fountain, since known as the " Fountain of Elisha," a view and description will be found in Part III. of this work. In Ezra, ii. 34. and Neh. vii. 36. we read, that three hundred and forty-five of the inhabitants of Jericho, who had been carried into captivity, returned to Judæa with Zerubbabel, and in Neh. iii. 2. we find them at work upon the walls of Jerusalem.

Jericho appears to have continued in a flourishing condition during several centuries. In the time of our Saviour it was inferior only to Jerusalem in the number and splendour of its public edifices, and was one of the royal residences of Herod misnamed the Great, who died there. It was situated in the hollow or bottom of the extensive plain called the " Great Plain," (which circumstance marks the propriety of the expression " going down to Jerusalem," in Luke, x. 30.) and is about nineteen miles distant from the capital of Judæa. In the last war of the Romans with the Jews, Jericho was sacked by Vespasian, and its inhabitants were put to the sword. Subsequently re-established by the emperor Hadrian, A. D. 138, it was doomed at no very distant period to experience new disasters : again was it repaired by the Christians, who made it an episcopal see ; but in the twelfth century it was captured by the Mohammedans, and has not since emerged from its ruins. Of all its magnificent buildings there remains part of only one tower, the dwelling of the governor of the district, which is seen on the left of our engraving, and which is traditionally said to have been the dwelling of Zaccheus the publican (who dwelt at Jericho, Luke, xix. 1, 2.), together with a quantity of rubbish which is supposed to mark the line of its antient walls. The sheds roughly constructed of boughs, which are seen in the foreground of our view, are the rude habitations of the wretched Arab inhabitants, who were there at the time our view was taken.

The steep mountainous ridge in the background of our engraving is called the Mountain of Quarantania, and is supposed to have been the scene of our Saviour's temptation. (Matt. iv. 1—10.) Here Dr. Shaw is of opinion that the two spies of Joshua concealed themselves. (Josh. ii. 16.) This mountain commands a distinct and delightful view of the mountains of Arabia, of the Dead Sea, and of the extensive and fertile plain of Jericho. According to Mr. Maundrell, Quarantania is a most miserable, dry, and barren place, consisting of rocky mountains so torn

Pt. 12.

and disordered, as if the earth had here suffered some great convulsion. On the left hand, looking down a steep valley, as he passed along, he saw ruins of small cells and cottages, the former habitations of hermits who had retired thither for penance and mortification; for which purpose a more comfortless and abandoned place could not be found in the whole earth. The particular mountainous precipice, whence " all the kingdoms of the world and the glory of them " were shown to Jesus Christ, is, as the evangelist describes it, " an exceeding high mountain" (Matt. iv. 8.), and in its ascent not only difficult but dangerous : it has a small chapel at the top, and another about half way down, founded on a projecting part of the rock. Near the latter are several caves and holes, excavated by the hermits, in which they kept their fast of Lent in imitation of that of Jesus Christ.

As Jericho was one of the cities appropriated to the residence of the priests and Levites (twelve thousand of whom are said to have dwelt there in the time of Jesus Christ), and as the way thither lay through the rocky desert, or wilderness of Jericho, the road antiently was, as it still is, greatly infested by robbers, who insult, stop, and plunder the traveller on his journey. A country more favourable to the attacks of predatory banditti, and caves better adapted for concealment than those presented on this road, can scarcely be imagined. These circumstances mark the admirable propriety with which our Lord made it the scene of his beautiful and instructive narrative of the benevolent Samaritan. (Luke, x. 30—37.) In this gorge Sir Frederick Henniker was attacked and severely wounded : a better place for such an attack could not be found, as half a dozen rifles would have sufficed to discomfit a host.

" The whole of this road," says Mr. Buckingham, " from Jerusalem to the Jordan, is held to be the most dangerous about Palestine ; and indeed, in this portion of it, the very aspect of the scenery is sufficient, on the one hand, to tempt to robbery and murder, and, on the other, to occasion a dread of it in those who pass that way. . . . . . . One must be amid these rude and gloomy solitudes, surrounded by an armed band, and feel the impatience of the traveller, who rushes on to catch a new view at every pass and turn ; one must be alarmed at the very tramp of the horses' hoofs rebounding through the caverned rocks, and at the savage shouts of the footmen, scarcely less loud than the echoing thunder produced by the discharge of their pieces in the valleys ; one must witness all this upon the spot, before the full force and beauty of the admirable story of the good Samaritan can be perceived. Here pillage, wounds, and death, would be accompanied with double terror, from the frightful aspect of every thing around. Here the unfeeling act of passing by a fellow-creature in distress, as the priest and Levite are said to have done, strikes one with horror as an act almost more than inhuman. And here, too, the compassion of the good Samaritan is doubly virtuous, from the purity of the motive which must have led to it, in a spot where no eyes were fixed upon him to draw forth the performance of any duty, and from the bravery which was necessary to admit of a man's exposing himself by such delay to the risk of a similar fate to that from which he was endeavouring to rescue his fellow-creature."

₊ Maundrell's Travels, pp. 106, 107. Dr. Shaw's Travels, vol. ii. pp. 36, 37. Carne's Letters from the East, pp. 321, 322. Dr. Richardson's Travels, vol. ii. pp. 395, 396. Russell's Palestine, pp. 256—262. Sir F. Henniker's Notes during a Visit to Egypt, &c. pp. 289—291. Buckingham's Travels in Palestine, pp. 292, 293.

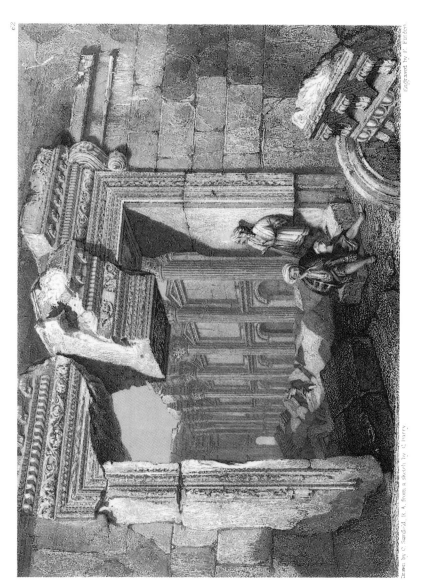

GATE AT BAALBEC.

(Baal-Gad or Baal-Hamon)

Drawn by C. Stanfield, R. A. from a sketch by C. Barry.

Engraved by E. Finden.

GATE AT BAALBEC

(BAAL-GAD, OR BAAL-HAMON).

Drawn by C. STANFIELD, from a Sketch made on the spot by CHARLES BARRY, Esq.

BAAL-GAD was situated " in the valley of Lebanon, under Mount Hermon" (Josh. xi. 17. xii. 7.), and was among the places unconquered by the Israelites at the death of Joshua (xiii. 5.). By the Greeks and Romans it was called Heliopolis, and by the modern natives Baalbec, both which names mean " the city of the sun." It was, perhaps, the place called Baal-Hamon in Sol. Song, viii. 11., and also Baalath in 1 Kings, ix. 18. The inhabitants of this country, — Mohammedans, Jews, and Christians, — all confidently believe that Baalbec was built by Solomon. Certain it is, that no Oriental monarch could indulge his favourite pleasures in a more luxurious retirement than among the streams and shades of Baalbec.

The magnificent GATE delineated in our engraving is the entrance to the Temple of the Sun, of which, and of the other remains of antient art at Baalbec, a descriptive account will be found in Part VII. of this work. It is constructed of marble, and the architrave is enriched with arabesque sculpture in high relief, and of exquisite workmanship. One band is composed of flowers and ears of corn; and another, of vine-leaves, with male and female dancers, and other figures, within the tendrils. On the underside of the lintel is a fine example of the Roman eagle in high relief, with genii on each side holding festoons of flowers hanging from the eagle's beak. The interior of the temple, seen through the doorway, is an exceedingly florid specimen of the Corinthian style of architecture. Engaged columns are in each wall, with intervening niches for statues; and at the entrance-end are indications of an arcade, forming a gallery.

Drawn by J.M.W. Turner, R.A. from a sketch by the Rev.ᵈ B. Masters

Engraved by E. Finden.

THE DEAD SEA, JERICHO AND THE MOUTH OF THE JORDAN.

The Mountains of Moab in the Distance.

JOSH. XV. 5.

THE DEAD SEA,

Drawn by J. M. W. TURNER, from a Sketch made on the spot by the Rev. ROBERT
M. MASTER.

THE celebrated lake, which occupies the site of Sodom and Gomorrah, is
variously called in Scripture the SEA OF THE PLAIN (Deut. iii. 17.
iv. 49.), being situated in a valley with a plain lying to the south of it,
where those cities once flourished, with the other cities of the plain; the
SALT SEA (Deut. iii. 17. Josh. xv. 5.), from the extremely saline and
bitter taste of its waters; the SALT SEA EASTWARD (Num. xxxiv. 3.)
and the EAST SEA (Ezek. xlvii. 18. Joel ii. 20.), from its situation
relatively to Judæa. At present it is called BAHRET-LOUT, or the Sea
of Lot. By Josephus and other writers, it was called the Lake ASPHAL-
TITES, from the abundance of bitumen found in it. The most familiar
name, the DEAD SEA, is in allusion to the antient tradition, erroneously
but generally received, that no animal can exist in its stagnant and hydro-
sulphuretted waters, which, though they look remarkably clear and pure,
are nauseous in the extreme. A chemical analysis of one hundred grains
of the water gave the following results as to the substances, and proportions of them, which it holds in solution : —

| Muriate of lime | - | 3·920 | Soda | - | - | 10·360 |
| Magnesia | - | - | 10·246 | Sulphate of lime | | | ·054 |

From this analysis it will readily be concluded that such a liquid must be
equally salt and bitter. The acrid saltness of its waters, indeed, is much
greater than that of the sea: and the land which surrounds this lake,
being equally impregnated with that saltness, refuses to produce any
plants, except a few stunted thorns, which wear the brown garb of the
desert. Bodies sink or float upon it in proportion to their specific gravity:
and although the water is so dense as to be favourable to swimmers, no
security is found against the common accident of drowning. This sea,
when viewed from the spot where the rapid Jordan daily discharges into
it 6,090,000 tons of muddy water, takes a south-easterly direction visible
for ten or fifteen miles, when it disappears in a curve towards the east.
In our engraving, the course of the Jordan is distinctly exhibited, and
contiguous to it appears the city of Jericho. The expanse of the Dead
Sea, at the embouchure of the Jordan, has been supposed not to exceed

five or six miles; though the mountains, which skirt each side of the
valley of the Dead Sea, are apparently separated by a distance of eight
miles. The mountains on the Judæan side (one of which is exhibited
on the right of our view) are lower than the MOUNTAINS OF MOAB, on
the Arabian side, which form a prominent feature in the distance. The
latter chain at its southern extremity is said to consist of dark granite,
and of various colours. The shores at the northern extremity are remarkably flat, and strewed with vast quantities of driftwood, white and
bleached by the sun, which is brought down by the swelling of Jordan.
It is not certainly known whether there has been any visible increase or
decrease in the waters of the Dead Sea. Some have imagined that it
finds a subterraneous passage to the Mediterranean, or that there is a
considerable suction in the plain which forms its western boundary; but
Dr. Shaw has long since accounted for it, by the quantity which is daily
evaporated.

As the Dead Sea advances towards the south, it evidently increases in
breadth. Its dimensions have been variously estimated by different travellers. Pliny states its total length to be one hundred miles, and its
greatest breadth twenty-five: the Jewish historian Josephus, who measured this lake, found that in length it extended about five hundred and
eighty stadia, and in breadth one hundred and fifty; according to our
standard, somewhat more than seventy miles by nineteen. With this
measurement nearly coincides the estimate of Dr. Shaw, who appears
to have ascertained its dimensions with accuracy, and who computes its
length to be about seventy-two English miles, and its greatest breadth
about nineteen. Whoever has once seen the Dead Sea, will ever after
have its aspect impressed upon his memory: it is in truth a gloomy and
fearful spectacle. The precipices, in general, descend abruptly into the
lake, the surface of which is generally unruffled, from the hollow of the
basin (in which it lies) scarcely admitting the free passage necessary for
a strong breeze. It is, however, for the same reason, subject to whirl-
winds or squalls of short duration. A profound silence, awful as death,
hangs over the lake: its shores are rarely visited by any footstep, save
that of the wild Arab; and its desolate but majestic features are well
suited to the tales related concerning it by the inhabitants of the country,
who hold it in superstitious dread, and speak of it with terror.

₊ The above description has been condensed from the researches of Buckingham,
Carne, Chateaubriand, Clarke, Jolliffe, Irby and Mangles, Maundrell, Russell, Shaw,
Wilson, and the anonymous author of " Three Weeks in Palestine."

Drawn by J. D. Harding, from an Original by Cassas.

Engraved by W. Finden.

RUINS OF TYRE.

EZEK. xxvi—xxviii

RUINS OF TYRE.

Drawn by J. D. HARDING, partly from a Sketch made on the spot by J. BONOMI, Esq., and partly from a View given in the French Work of LAS CASAS.

TYRE was the most celebrated city of Phœnicia, and the theatre of an immense commerce and navigation. Tyre was twofold, insular and continental: Tyre on the island succeeded to the more antient city on the continent, which was called *Palæ-Tyrus*, or Old Tyre. Though inferior to Sidon in point of antiquity, Palæ-Tyrus soon rose above it, and became the richest mart of the antient world. In Josh. xix. 29. it is called the " strong city, Tyre," and in 2 Sam. xxiv. 7. the " strong hold of Tyre." In reference to its antiquity, Isaiah (xxiii. 7.) calls it " a city whose antiquity is of antient days." From Hiram, king of Tyre, Solomon obtained timber, gold, and workmen for the building of the temple. Hiram also sent his ships with those of Solomon to Ophir and Tarshish. (1 Kings, ix. 10—14. 27. x. 22.) In later times the friendship of the Tyrians and Jews seems to have been interrupted, whence the prophets Amos and Joel speak of Tyre as of a hostile city. (Amos, i. 9, 10. Joel, iii. 4.)

At the time of the Assyrian invasion under Shalmaneser, Old Tyre had arrived to such a pitch of opulence and splendour, that Isaiah speaks of it as the "joyous city.... the crowning city, whose merchants are princes, whose traffickers are the honourable of the earth." (xxiii. 7, 8.) It was afterwards taken by Nebuchadnezzar (whose forces it withstood for thirteen years); but not until the Tyrians had removed their effects to the insular town, and left nothing but the bare walls to the victor, by whom they were demolished. The fate of Tyre is the subject of numerous predictions. See particularly Isa. xxiii. Jer. xxv. Ezek. xxvi—xxviii. Amos, i. 9, 10. and Zech. ix. 1—8.

While this mart of nations was in the height of its opulence and power, and at least one hundred and twenty-five years before the destruction of Old Tyre, Isaiah pronounced its irrevocable fall; and as insular Tyre succeeded to Palæ-Tyrus, being inhabited by the same people (whose wickedness, exultation over the calamities of the Jews, and their cruelty in selling them for slaves, are assigned as the reasons of the impending judgments), the fate of both is included in the prophecy.

The predictions of the prophets above referred to were extremely minute and circumstantial, and announced that this city was to be taken and destroyed by the Chaldæans (who, when the prophecy was delivered, were an inconsiderable people), and particularly by Nebuchadnezzar; that the inhabitants should flee over the Mediterranean into the islands and countries adjoining, and even there should not find a quiet settlement; that the city should be restored after seventy years, and return to her gain and merchandise; that it should be taken and destroyed a second time; that the people should, in time, forsake their idolatry, and become converts to the worship and true religion of God; and, finally, that the city should be totally destroyed, and become a place only for fishers to spread their nets upon. Bishop Newton has proved how minutely these various predictions were fulfilled, to whose valuable Dissertations on the Prophecies the reader is necessarily referred. Yet a few of the most striking predictions, the fulfilment of which rests on the most unexceptionable testimony, may be selected.

" One of the most singular events in history was the manner in which the siege of Tyre was conducted by Alexander the Great. Irritated that a single city should alone oppose his victorious march, enraged at the murder of some of his soldiers, and fearful for his fame, — even his army's despairing of success could not deter him from the siege. And Tyre was taken in a manner, the success of which was more wonderful than the design was daring; for it was surrounded by a wall one hundred and fifty feet in height, and situated on an island half a mile distant from the shore. A mound was formed from the continent to the island; and the ruins of old Tyre, two hundred and forty years after its demolition, afforded ready materials for the purpose. Such was the work, that the attempts at first defeated the power of an Alexander. The enemy consumed and the storm destroyed it. But its remains, buried beneath the water, formed a barrier which rendered successful his renewed efforts. A vast mass of additional matter was requisite. The soil and the very rubbish were gathered and heaped. And the mighty conqueror, who afterwards failed in raising again any of the ruins of Babylon, cast those of Tyre into the sea, and took her very DUST from off her. He left not the remnant of a ruin — and the site of ancient Tyre is now unknown. Who then taught the prophets to say of Tyre — ' They shall lay thy stones, and thy timber, and thy dust, in the midst of the water — I will also SCRAPE HER DUST from her. I will make thee a terror, and thou shalt be no more. Thou shalt be sought for, yet thou shalt never be found again.' (Ezek. xxiv. 4. 12. 21.)

" After the capture of Tyre, the conqueror ordered it to be set on fire. Fifteen thousand of the Tyrians escaped in ships; and, exclusive of multitudes that were cruelly slain, thirty thousand were sold into slavery. Each of these facts had been announced for centuries: — ' Behold the Lord will cast her out — he will smite her power in the sea, and she shall be devoured with fire. — I will bring forth a fire from the midst of thee — I will bring thee to ashes upon the earth. Pass ye over to Tarshish — pass over to Chittim. The isles that are in the sea shall be troubled at thy departure. — Thou shalt die the death of them that are slain in the midst of the sea. The children of Israel also, and the children of Judah have ye sold. I will return the recompence upon your own head.'

" But it was also prophesied, — ' I will make thee like the top of a rock. Thou shalt be a place to spread nets upon.' (Ezek. xxvi. 14, 15.) The same prediction is repeated, with an assurance of its truth: — ' I will make her like the top of a rock; it shall be a place for the spreading of nets in the midst of the sea, for I have spoken it.' (Ezek. xxvi. 5.)

" Tyre, though deprived of its former inhabitants, soon revived as a city, and greatly regained its commerce. It was populous and flourishing at the beginning of the Christian era. It contained many disciples of Jesus, in the days of the apostles. An elegant temple and many churches were afterwards built there. It was the see of the first archbishop under the patriarch of Jerusalem. Her merchandise and her hire, according to the prophecy, were holiness to the Lord. In the seventh century Tyre was taken by the Saracens; in the twelfth by the crusaders — at which period it was a great commercial city. The Mamelukes succeeded as its masters; and it has now remained for three hundred years in the possession of the Turks. But it was not excluded from among the multitude of cities and of countries whose ruin and devastation, as accomplished by the cruelties and ravages of Turkish barbarity and despotism, were foretold nearly two thousand years before the existence of that nation of plunderers. And although it has more lately, by a brief respite from the greatest oppression, risen somewhat from its ruins, the last of the predictions respecting it has been literally fulfilled," according to the unanimous testimony of modern travellers.

From these accounts it appears that modern Tyre (now called Soor) is situated at the extremity of a sandy peninsula, and covers a space about one mile in length, and half a mile in breadth. Its appearance has nothing of magnificence. Its small port is choked up with sand and rubbish, so that the boats of the fishermen who visit this once renowned emporium, and dry their nets upon its rocks and ruins, cannot be admitted without great difficulty. According to Mr. Buckingham, the place now contains about 800 stone buildings; but Mr. Rae Wilson reduces this number to 200. The population has been variously stated, by different travellers, at 1700, 4000, and from 5000 to 8000. The causes of these discrepancies it falls not within the plan of this work to account for. The commerce of Tyre with Alexandria, which consists chiefly of silk and tobacco, is very trifling. Numerous beautiful columns stretched along the beach, or standing in fragments half buried in the sand, which has been accumulating for ages (of which our engraving will afford some idea), still exist, — an affecting monument of the fragile and transitory nature of earthly grandeur.

⁎ Bishop Newton on the Prophecies, Dissertation xi. Keith on Prophecy, pp. 340—343. Maundrell's Travels, p. 38. Pococke's Description of the East, vol. ii. book i. p. 83. Shaw's Travels, vol. ii. pp. 30, 31. Jolliffe's Letters from Palestine, p. 13. (1820.) Rae Wilson's Travels, vol. ii. pp. 64—66. Jowett's Christian Researches in the Mediterranean, pp. 131—141. Irby's and Mangles' Travels, pp. 197, 198. Buckingham's Travels in Palestine, vol. i. pp. 52. 73—76.

Drawn by A.W Callcott. R.A from a sketch by Sir A.Edmonstone, & A Allen. Esq

THE FORDS OF THE JORDAN.

Engraved by E Finden.

THE FORDS OF THE JORDAN.

Drawn by A. W. Callcott, from a Sketch made on the Spot by
the Rev. R. Master and A. Allen, Esq.

. . . . " The fords of Jordan."—*Judg.* iii. 28.

The Jordan is the principal river of Palestine: it derives its name (*Jor* or *Yar-dan*, the River of Dan) because its rise was in the vicinity of the little city of Dan. Its true source is in two fountains at Paneas, a city better known by its subsequent name of Cæsarea Philippi, at the foot of Anti-Libanus. Its apparent source flows from beneath a cave, at the foot of a precipice, in the sides of which are several niches, with Greek inscriptions. During many hours of its course, it continues to be a small and insignificant rivulet. It flows due south through the centre of the country, intersecting the lake Merom, antiently called Somonochitis, and the sea of Galilee; and it loses itself in the Dead Sea: though it is probable that in very antient times it pursued its course to the Red Sea, until the convulsions occasioned by the destruction of Sodom and Gomorrah, and the subsequent filling up of the bottom of the valley by the drifting sand, caused the stoppage of its waters.

The course of this river is almost one hundred miles: its breadth and depth are various. Dr. Shaw computed it to be about thirty yards broad, and three yards or nine feet in depth. Messrs. Bankes and Buckingham, who crossed it in 1816, pretty nearly at the same ford over which the Israelites passed on their first entering the promised land, found the stream extremely rapid. Its depth here is stated to be not more than four feet. This ford is delineated in our engraving; and in the foreground are pilgrims collected for the purpose of bathing in its hallowed waters. The annual procession for this purpose takes place after the festival of Easter. The pilgrims quit the Holy City under the protection of the governor of Jerusalem and his guards, who defend them from the assaults of the plundering Arabs of the district. The journey and ceremony of bathing in the river generally occupy the greater part of three days; though many of the travellers perform it in two. The stream flows between steep banks, overshadowed by willows and other shrubs. After riding along the bank for about two miles, and passing through a thicket of tamarisks and oleanders, at a bend of the river

Pt. 4.

thickly shaded with willows, the pilgrims reach the spot delineated in our view; they then immediately strip, and, rushing down the steep bank, plunge into the sacred stream. Many carry with them a white robe, to wear at this ceremony. When they are clothed again, and have filled their bottles with the holy water, they return to Jerusalem.

⁎ Irby's and Mangle's Travels, pp. 287—289. 329, 330.; Maundrell's Travels, p. 110.; Richardson's Travels, vol. ii. p. 387, 388.; Three Weeks in Palestine, pp. 89, 90.; Carne's Recollections, p. 38.; Shaw's Travels, vol. ii. pp. 156, 157.; Buckingham's Travels, p. 315.

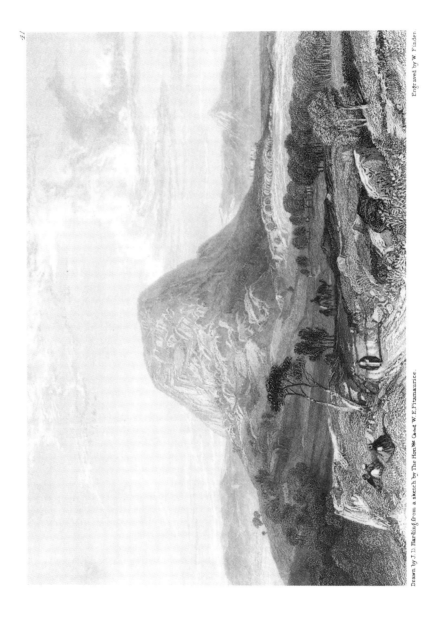

41

Drawn by J. D. Harding from a sketch by The Hon.ble Capt. W. E. Fitzmaurice.

Engraved by W. Finden.

MOUNT TABOR.

JUDGES IV. 6. 12.

MOUNT TABOR.

Drawn by J. D. Harding, from a Sketch made on the spot by the Hon. Capt. Fitzmaurice.

MOUNT TABOR, or THABOR, as it is sometimes called, is a calcareous mountain of a conical form, entirely detached from any neighbouring mountain : it stands on one side of the great plain of Esdraelon. The sides are rugged and precipitous, and covered to the summit with the most beautiful shrubs and flowers. Here Barak was encamped when, at the suggestion of the prophetess Deborah, he descended with ten thousand men, and discomfited the host of Sisera. (Judg. iv. 6, &c.) And, long afterwards, Hosea reproached the princes of Israel and the priests of the golden calves with having " been a snare in Mizpeh and a net spread upon Tabor" (Hos. v. 1.), doubtless referring to the altars and idols which were here set up ; and on this " high mountain apart" the transfiguration of Jesus Christ is generally believed to have taken place. (Matt. xvii. 1, 2.) Tabor is computed to be about a mile in height. To a person standing at its foot, it appears to terminate in a point : but, on reaching the top, he is agreeably surprised to find an oval plain, about a quarter of a mile in its greatest length, covered with a bed of fertile soil on the west, and having on its eastern side a mass of ruins, apparently the vestiges of churches, grottoes, and strong walls, all decidedly of some antiquity, and a few appearing to be the works of a very remote age. The Hon. Capt. Fitzmaurice, who visited this mountain in February, 1833, states that he saw the ruins of a very antient church, built over the spot where the transfiguration is supposed to have taken place.

The prospects from the summit of Mount Tabor are singularly delightful and extensive. On the north-west, says Mr. Buckingham, (whose graphic description has been confirmed by subsequent travellers), " we had a view of the Mediterranean Sea, whose blue surface filled up an open space left by a downward bend in the outline of the western hills : to the west-north-west a small portion of its waters were seen ; and on the west, again, the slender line of the distant horizon was just perceptible over the range of land near the sea-coast. From the west to the south, the plain of Esdraelon extended over a vast space, being bounded on the south by a range of hills generally considered to be Hermon, whose dews

Pt. 10.

are poetically celebrated (Psal. cxxxiii. 3.), and having in the same direction, nearer the foot of Tabor, the springs of Ain-el-Sherar, which send a perceptible stream through its centre, and form the brook Kishon of antiquity. From the south-east to the east is the plain of Galilee, being almost a continuation of Esdraelon, and, like it, appearing to be highly cultivated. Beneath the range of Hermon is seated Endor, famed for the witch who raised the ghost of Samuel (1 Sam. xxviii.), and Nain, equally celebrated as the place at which Jesus raised to life the only son of a widow, and restored him to his afflicted parent. The range which bounds the eastern view is thought to be the ' mountains of Gilboa,' so fatal to Saul. (1 Sam. xxxi.) The Sea of Tiberias, or Lake of Gennesareth, is clearly discovered towards the north-east, and somewhat farther in this direction is pointed out the village of Saphet, anciently named Bethulia, the city alluded to by Jesus Christ in his divine sermon on the Mount, from which it is also very conspicuous.

"The rest of this glorious panorama comprehends the sublime ' Mount of Beatitudes,' upon which that memorable sermon was delivered, together with the route to Damascus, and, lastly, Mount Lebanon, towering in the background in prodigious grandeur, the summit of which is covered with perpetual snow."

₊ Jolliffe's Letters from Palestine, p. 140. Buckingham's Travels in Palestine, pp. 107—109. Dr. E. D. Clarke's Travels in Greece, &c. vol. iv. p. 238. Rae Wilson's Travels, vol. ii. pp. 32—35. The Hon. Capt. Fitzmaurice's (unpublished) Cruise to Egypt, Palestine, and Greece, p. 58.

Drawn by Thomas for Capt. E. Fitzmaurice from a sketch taken on the spot.

Engraved by E. Finden.

BROOK KISHON.

The River of Kishon swept them away, that antient river.

JUDGES V. 21.

THE RIVER KISHON,

AND

PART OF MOUNT CARMEL.

Sketched and drawn by the Hon. Capt. W. E. FITZMAURICE.

THE KISHON is a celebrated river in the land of Israel, which, according to the united testimony of antient authors and of modern travellers (with the exception of Dr. Shaw), takes its rise near the foot of Mount Tabor. Its course is at first southerly; and as it passes through the plain of Esdraelon, it receives the waters which descend from the circumjacent mountains. At the south-west corner of that plain the Kishon reaches the foot of Mount Carmel; and then, flowing to the north-west, between its base and the hills on the north, it discharges itself into the Mediterranean Sea at the port of Acre.

Several important events are recorded to have taken place near this river. The battle between Barak and Sisera was fought in this region, probably after the river had been swollen by torrents which descended after a thunder-storm. Hence Deborah in her triumphant song says:— "They fought from heaven, the stars in their courses fought against Sisera. The river of Kishon swept them away, that antient river, the River Kishon." (Judg. v. 20, 21.) When the prophet Elijah had convinced the Israelites that Jehovah was the true God, he commanded them to seize the prophets of Baal, and bring them down to the Brook Kishon, where they were put to death. (1 Kings xviii. 40.) When Maundrell saw this river, in March, 1697, its waters were low and inconsiderable; but, in passing along the side of the plain, he discerned the traces of many small torrents falling down into it from the mountains, which must necessarily make it swell exceedingly after sudden rains. Dr. Pococke forded it early in the eighteenth century. In the beginning of September, 1815, the German traveller, Otho von Richter, rode through the clear green water of the Mukattua (Kishon), which, he states, at its mouth divides itself into several arms, and irrigates several charming gardens. When this region was visited by the Hon. Captain FITZMAURICE, in March, 1833, " the river was much swollen, in consequence of the mountain rains, and came tumbling down through the

Pt. 6.

rocks like distant thunder. The consequence of this," he continues, " was, that we were obliged to strip, tie our clothes on the top of our saddles, and alternately swim and ford with the horses." This is the scene delineated in our engraving. After passing the river, his road lay along the foot of Mount Carmel, which is wooded from the top to the bottom with most beautiful shrubs, interspersed with a variety of flowers. " In many places there were men transplanting the olive trees, which seemed to grow in wild profusion. There is abundance of game all over the mountain; wild boars, gazelles, and hares find shelter in the under-wood, and all the streams swarm with every species of water-fowl. At the extremity of the range is a strong exemplification of the prophecy of Amos (i. 2.) that ' the top of Carmel should wither:' and the barren aspect of the headland, which stretches out into the sea, and forms one horn of the bay of Acre, is in singular contrast with the rich verdure" of other parts of the mountain.

    *** Maundrell's Travels, p. 76.   Biblical Repository (Andover, Massachussetts, vol. i. pp. 601, 602.)   Hon. Capt. Fitzmaurice's (unpublished) Cruise to Egypt, Palestine, and Greece, p. 62.

Drawn by the Hon.ble Capt.n Fitzmaurice.

Engraved by W. Finden.

THE PLAIN OF JEZREEL OR ESDRAELON.

Drawn from Jenin.

JUDGES VI. 33.

THE PLAIN OF JEZREEL, OR OF ESDRAELON,

FROM MODIN.

Drawn on the spot by the Hon. W. E. FITZMAURICE.

THE PLAIN OF JEZREEL, or of ESDRAELON, is an extensive level of Palestine, which extends from Mount Carmel and the Mediterranean, through the middle of the Holy Land, to the place where the river Jordan issues from the Sea of Tiberias. Antiently, it was called the " Valley of Jezreel," (Judg. vi. 33.); sometimes it is named the " Great Plain," and the " Plain of Tabor." Here, in the most fertile part of the land of Canaan the tribe of Issachar " rejoiced in their tents." (Deut. xxxiii. 18.)

In all ages it seems to have been most distinguished as a theatre for local war: it certainly is well adapted for an extensive force, being about twenty-five miles long, and varying from six to fourteen in breadth. On this spot it was that the host of Sisera fell on the edge of the sword before Barak, who came down upon them like a torrent from Mount Tabor, with an overwhelming army. (Judg. iv. 13—16.) Here also Josiah, king of Judah, fought in disguise against Pharaoh Necho, king of Egypt, and fell by the arrows of his antagonist (2 Kings, xxiii. 29.); and here Nebuchadnezzar encamped with his mighty host against the nations, in revenge for their having refused to idolise him. Jews, Gentiles, Saracens, Christian crusaders, and anti-christian Frenchmen, Egyptians, Persians, Druses, Turks, and Arabs, warriors out of every nation under heaven, have pitched their tents in the Plain of Esdraelon, and have beheld the various banners of their nation wet with the dews of Tabor and of Hermon. The last battle which was fought here, called by some the battle of Esdraelon, and by others that of Mount Tabor, was in the spring of 1799, between fifteen hundred Frenchmen under the command of General Kleber and an army of several thousand Turks and Mamelukes, who fought most gallantly until the very last ball was expended, when Buonaparte attacked them with a corps de reserve, and completely discomfited them.

The plain of Esdraelon is inclosed on all sides by mountains ; — by the
Pt. 21.

hills of Nazareth to the north, those of Samaria to the south, the mountains of Tabor and Hermon to the east, and by Carmel to the south-west. Although it bears the title of " Plain," yet it abounds with hills, which, in the view of it from the adjacent mountains, shrink into nothing. Here, if there were perfect security from the government (a thing unknown for centuries), it has been computed that, where only five wretched villages were seen, twenty-five good towns might stand, at a distance of three miles from one another, each with a population of a thousand souls, to the great improvement of the cultivation of so bountiful a soil. The Hon. Captain Fitzmaurice, in February, 1833, observed but little or no cultivation going on; though in some places, where the plain was intersected with water-courses, the horses frequently sank half way up to their shoulders in the rich loamy soil. Cotton is raised here, the quality of which is supposed to be superior to any in the east. The fruitfulness of this plain is in a great degree to be attributed to the river Kishon, which flows through it.

*** Dr. Clarke's Travels, vol. iv. pp. 255—258. Rae Wilson's Travels in the Holy Land, &c. vol. i. pp. 382, 383. Jowett's Christian Researches in Syria, pp. 191, 192, 302. The Hon. Capt. Fitzmaurice's (unpublished) Cruise to Egypt, Palestine, and Greece, p. 77.

THE WILDERNESS OF ENGEDI.

And the Convent of Santa Saba.

1 SAM^s XXIV 1

Drawn by J. M. W. Turner, R.A. from a sketch by C. Barry, Esqr

Engraved by J. B. Allen.

THE WILDERNESS OF ENGEDI,

AND THE

CONVENT OF SANTA SABA.

Drawn by J. M. W. TURNER, from a Sketch by C. BARRY, Esq.

THE Hill of Engedi is about six miles distant from Jerusalem. Engedi is low towards the north, but descends steep into the WILDERNESS on the south, on which side of it, not far beneath the summit, is the cave where Saul and David reposed, when the latter so magnanimously spared the life of his inveterate enemy. (1 Sam. xxiv. 1—18.) At first, it appears neither lofty nor spacious; but a low passage on the left leads into apartments, where a party could easily remain concealed from those without. The face of the hill around it corresponds to the description given of Saul going in pursuit of David: — He " went to seek David and his men upon the rocks of the wild goats." (1 Sam. xxiv. 2.) The way through the wilderness is very wild. The hills, over which it leads, are in general covered with coarse grass, and in some parts composed of sand. They are intersected by deep and narrow ravines, filled with wild verdure, in the sides of which are several caverns. The place is well calculated to afford secure concealment from pursuit amidst its recesses, or " strong-holds," as it did to David when pursued by Saul. (1 Sam. xxiii. 29.)

At the extremity of this wilderness stands the convent of Santa Saba, which was founded in the sixth century: it is erected on the summit of a ravine three or four hundred feet deep, at the bottom of which flows the brook Kedron. This brook generally has but little water, and often none; but after storms or heavy rains it swells and runs with much impetuosity. The church stands on a small eminence at the bottom of the dell: it is a very antient structure, adorned with grotesque figures of old male and female saints. The buildings of the monastery rise above it by an almost perpendicular flight of steps cut out of the rock, and thus ascend to the ridge of the hill, where they terminate in two square towers. The dome which appears near the centre of our engraving contains the tomb of Saint Saba, by whom the monastic and eremitical life was here instituted in the fourth century. Not fewer than ten thousand recluses

Pt. 6.

are said to have dwelt within this convent at one time; but not more than thirty Greek monks are at present resident, whose industry is very conspicuous. Flights of stone steps conduct to several small terraces, one above another; and from below they have conveyed a portion of the soil to these terraces, on which they cultivate a variety of vegetables for the use of the convent. In a dark and cavernous apartment is a very extraordinary spectacle: the opposite sides of the precipices are full of caves: a great number of Christians were slaughtered here by a body of soldiers sent by one of the caliphs; and the skulls of those martyrs have been collected in this chamber, in which they have been piled in small pyramids, to the number of two or three thousand. From the roof of the convent a flight of steps leads to a narrow wooden tower, which over-looks the wilderness to a great distance, having the deep glen of the Kedron far beneath, and commanding a view of the Dead Sea. Here a monk is often stationed, to give notice of the approach of any of the wild Arabs who dwell there. As at the convent of Mount Sinai, these fellows come to the foot of the walls, and clamorously demand bread. A large quantity of small brown cakes is always kept in the tower for these occasions; they are thrown out of the window to the Arabs, who then depart. According to Dr. Pococke, this convent possesses such privileges, that no Mohammedan can enter it, under a penalty of five hundred dollars, payable to the mosque at Jerusalem. In this retirement dwelt John of Damascus, Euphemius, Cyril of Jerusalem, — saints of distinguished eminence in the martyrology of the Greek church.

⁎ Pococke's Description of the East, vol. ii. p. 34.   Carne's Letters from the East, pp. 307—313.   Chateaubriand, Itinéraire, p. 160.

57.

Engraved by W. Finden.

Drawn by G. Balmer, from a sketch on the spot by F. Catherwood, Esq.ʳ

MOUNT ZION, JERUSALEM.

(The Mosque of David.)

2 SAM. V. 6. 9.   1ˢᵗ KINGS II. 10.   MATT III. 12.

JERUSALEM.

MOUNT ZION — THE MOSQUE OF DAVID.

Drawn by F. Catherwood, from a Sketch made on the spot by George Bulmer, Esq.

Mount Zion or Sion is one of the mountains on which the southern quarter of antient Jerusalem was built, (though the greater part of it is now without the walls of the city,) and on which the citadel of the Jebusites stood, when David took possession of it, and transferred his court thither from Hebron. (2. Sam. v. 6—9.) Hence it is frequently called the city of David (2 Sam. v. 9. vi. 10. 12. 1 Kings, viii. 1.), who was interred here. (1 Kings, ii. 10.) Over his tomb and on the middle of this mount is erected the long dingy-looking Turkish mosque delineated in our engraving, which appears to be of considerable antiquity. It is called the mosque of the prophet David, whose reputed tomb is still exhibited in the interior, and is held in the greatest possible veneration by the Mussulmans, by whom it is guarded with great vigilance. The santones belonging to this mosque are the most powerful in Jerusalem. Part of this building is said to have been the church of the cœnaculum, where our Saviour ate the last supper with his disciples. Dr. Richardson was shown into an upper room in the front of the building, which, it was affirmed, was the identical room in which the Lord's Supper was instituted. Unhappily for this tradition, thirty-nine years after, not only the wall but every house in Jerusalem was rased from the foundations, and the ground ploughed up by the Roman soldiers.

" Mount Zion is considerably higher than the ground on the north, on which the antient city stood, or that on the east, leading on to the Valley of Jehoshaphat ; but as it has very little relative height above the ground on the south and on the west, it must have owed its boasted strength principally to a deep ravine by which it is encompassed on the east, south, and west, and the strong, high walls and towers, by which it was inclosed and flanked completely round. This ravine or valley (more correctly, trench or ditch) seems to have been formed by art on the south and west, the surface of the ground on each side being of nearly equal height, though Mount Zion is certainly the highest ; yet so little that it could not have derived much strength from the elevation." The

Pt. 14.

breadth of this ditch is nearly one hundred and fifty feet, and its depth, or the height of Mount Zion above the bottom of the ravine, about sixty feet. The bottom of it is rock, covered with a thin sprinkling of earth; and in the winter season is the natural channel for conveying off the water that falls into it from the higher ground; but, on both sides, the rock is cut perpendicularly down, and most probably it was the quarry from which the greater part of the stones were taken for building the city. The precipitous edge of the ravine is more covered with earth on the side of Mount Zion than on the other side, which is probably owing to the barbarous custom of rasing cities from their foundation, and tumbling both earth and stone into the ditch below. The loose stones have all been removed from it, for building the present city.

When Dr. Richardson visited this mountain in 1818, " one part of it supported a crop of barley: another was undergoing the labour of the plough, and the soil turned up consisted of stone and lime mixed with earth, such as is usually met with in the foundations of ruined cities. It is nearly a mile in circumference, is highest on the west side, and towards the east falls down in broad terraces on the upper part of the mountain, and narrow ones on the side as it slopes down towards the brook Kedron. Each terrace is divided from the one above it by a low wall of dry stone, built of the ruins of this celebrated spot. The terraces near the bottom of the hill are still used as gardens, and are watered from the pool of Siloam. They belong chiefly to the inhabitants of the small village of Siloa, immediately opposite. We have here another remarkable instance of the special fulfilment of prophecy : — ' Therefore shall Zion for your sakes be ploughed as a field, and Jerusalem shall become heaps.' (Mal. iii. 12.)"

, Dr. Richardson's Travels, vol. ii. pp. 345—350.

Drawn by F. Catherwood.   Engraved by E. Finden.

JERUSALEM.

Pulpit on the platform of the Mosque of Omar.

JER.M. XII. 7.

JERUSALEM.

THE MOSQUE OF OMAR,

ERECTED ON MOUNT MORIAH, WHERE SOLOMON'S TEMPLE STOOD.

Drawn by D. ROBERTS from a Sketch made on the spot by F. CATHERWOOD, Esq.

THIS splendid building, which forms a conspicuous object in Mr. Catherwood's panoramic drawing of Jerusalem, occupies the site of the antient temple erected by Solomon on " mount Moriah, where the Lord appeared unto David his father in the place that David had prepared in the threshing floor of Ornan," or Araunah, "the Jebusite." (1 Kings, vi. with 2 Chron. iii. 1.) It was erected by the caliph Omar, and by the Moslems is reputed to be next in sanctity to the temple at Mecca. When Jerusalem was taken by the crusaders, it was converted into a Christian church; and when they finally abandoned the city, the victorious sultan Saladin caused the whole building to be washed with rosewater, by way of purification, before he would enter it.

The Mosque, which is the finest piece of Saracenic architecture in existence, is a regular octagon, each side being seventy feet in width; it is entered by four spacious doors facing the cardinal points, the Bab el Garb on the west, Bab nebbe Daoud, or Gate of David, on the east, Bab el Kebla, or the Gate of Prayer, on the south, and Bab el Djinna, or the Gate of Heaven, on the north; each of these entrances has a porch of timber-work, of considerable height, excepting Bab el Kebla, which has a fine portico, supported by eight Corinthian pillars of marble; the lower part of the walls is faced with marble, evidently very antient; it is white, with a slight tinge of blue, and pieces wholly blue are occasionally introduced with good effect; each face is panelled, the sides of the panels forming plain pilasters at the angles; the upper part is faced with small glazed tiles, about eight inches square, of various colours, blue being the prevailing, with passages from the Koran on them, forming a singular and beautiful mosaic; the four plain sides have each seven well-proportioned windows of stained glass; the four sides of entrance have only six. The roof gently rises towards the perpendicular part under the dome, which is also covered with coloured tiles, arranged in various elegant devices. The dome is double; it was built by Solyman I., of a spherical form; is covered with lead, and crowned by a gilt crescent; the whole is ninety feet in height, and has a light and beautiful effect: the fanciful disposition of the soft colours above, contrasting with the blue and white marble below, is extremely pleasing.

The interior is paved with grey marble; and the walls, which are quite plain, are covered with the same material, of a fine white colour. Twenty-four pillars of marble, of a brownish colour, form a concentric nave; the eight opposite the angles are square, without ornament; the other sixteen, being two to each face of the octagon, are round, well-proportioned, and about twenty feet in height, with capitals of a composite style, gilt; above is a plain plinth, and twenty-four small arches supporting the roof, which is wrought in compartments, and gilt in exquisite taste. A second circle of sixteen pillars, four square and twelve round, based on an elevation in the floor, to which there is an ascent of four steps, and having capitals, a plinth, and arches, as before, supports the dome, the interior of which is finely painted and gilt in arabesque; from the centre are suspended several antique vessels of gold and silver, offerings of some pious Mohammedans. Immediately beneath the dome, surrounded by a high iron railing, gilt, with only one gate of entrance, is an immense mass of limestone, of an irregular form, probably part of the rock on which the Mosque stands; it is named El Hadjera el Sahhara Allah, the Locked-up

Stone of God, and is held in the highest veneration. The tradition respecting it is, that it fell from heaven when the spirit of prophecy commenced; that all the antients to whom it was given prophesied from it; and that on this rock sat the angel of death, who, upon David's inconsiderate numbering of the people, slaughtered until God " commanded him to put up his sword again into the sheath thereof." (1 Chron. xxi. 7.) At the time the prophets fled from Jerusalem, the stone wished to accompany them, but was prevented by the angel Gabriel, who forcibly held it (the marks of his fingers still remain) until the arrival of Mohammed, who, by his prayers, fixed it for ever to the spot. Mohammed, in the twelfth year of his mission, made his celebrated night journey from Mecca to Jerusalem on the Beast el Borak, accompanied by the angel Gabriel, as described in the 17th chapter of the Koran; and having paid his devotions, ascended from this stone to heaven; the rock, sensible of the happiness, became soft, and the print of the prophet's foot remains to this day, an object of great veneration to all true believers. Some years back a portion of the rock was stolen by the Christians: but no sooner had they got it out of the Mosque than it became invisible to them, and was afterwards discovered by the Mussulmans. The rock is enclosed by a low wooden railing, and covered by a canopy of green and red satin; immediately beneath it is a natural chamber, called the " Ennobled Cavern of God," an irregular square chamber eighteen feet each way, and eight in the highest part, above which is a hole through the rock, called the " Hole of Mohammed." Five small cavities around are inscribed as the places of Solomon, David, Abraham, Gabriel, and St. John. It also contains the Well of Souls, or entrance to the infernal regions. This Mosque further contains the praying place and footstep of our Lord Idris; the praying place, sword (fourteen feet long), and standard of Ali, nephew of Mohammed; the scales for weighing the souls of men; the shield of Mohammed; the birds of Solomon; the pomegranates of David; and the saddle of El Borak; on a wooden desk, an original copy of the Koran, the leaves of which are four feet in length. In the outer circle there is a well, at which believers wash and drink; and near the western entrance is a slab of green marble, forming part of the floor, which has the marks of having been pierced by eighteen nails of silver; three of these and a portion of a fourth only remain, the others having at different times disappeared, in order to mark the completion of certain great epochs. The remainder are to follow; and when the last takes its departure, the fulness of time will be complete and the world end. It is also said that the nails were pulled out by the devil, in his attempts to enter paradise by this door.

This Mosque belongs especially to the principal and most respected Mussulman sect, that of the Hanifites (so called from Hanifah its founder), and has been kept sacred from the approach of Christians until very recently. Here, and in the Mosque at Mecca, the Mussulman believes his prayers to be more acceptable to God than any where else. It is believed by the Moslems that all the prophets, since the time of Adam, have come here to pray and prophesy; and that even now they come in invisible troops, accompanied by angels, to pray on the Sahhara. The usual guard of this holy stone is 70,000 angels, who are relieved every day. One hundred and eighty lamps are lighted at night in this Mosque.

✱ Travels of Ali Bey, vol. ii. pp. 214—218. Dr. Richardson's Travels, vol. ii. pp. 294—304. Communication from F. Catherwood, Esq.—Mr. C. has just published a very interesting Plan of Jerusalem. It is by far the most accurate representation of the position and buildings of that memorable city which has yet appeared; the greater part having been laid down from observations actually made by himself and by a German traveller who preceded him.

Drawn by C. Stanfield, A.R.A. from a view by C.R. Wood.

Engraved by E. Finden.

TADMOR IN THE DESERT.

1. KINGS IX. 18

TADMOR IN THE DESERT.

Drawn by C. STANFIELD, from a Sketch made on the spot by C. R. WOOD.

" TADMOR in the Wilderness," we learn from 1 Kings ix. 18. and 2 Chron. viii. 4., was erected by Solomon, King of the Hebrews ; who, according to Josephus (Ant. Jud. lib. viii. c. 6. § 1.), making an incursion into the desert, possessed himself of it, and there built a very great city, which he encompassed with strong walls, and gave to it the name of Thadamora, by which name it was called by the Syrians in his day ; but the Greeks denominated it Palmyra, from the abundance of *palm* trees.   He further states, as a reason for Solomon's erection of this city, that springs and wells of water were found in that place only ; and adds, that it is one day's journey from the Euphrates, two from Upper Syria, and six from Babylon.   It is probable that Solomon built it in order to facilitate his commerce with the East.   The original name was preserved until the time of Alexander, who extended his conquests to this city, which then exchanged Tadmor for Palmyra.   It was important, as the bulwark of Judæa against the incursions of the wandering tribes of the Euphrates : and its intermediate position between Mesopotamia and Syria, made it an excellent place of interchange for the commerce of the Mediterranean and the Indian Ocean.   The protection of its deserts for a long time secured its independence, and enabled it to maintain a friendly inter-course with each of the neighbouring and rival empires.

Palmyra submitted to the Romans about the year A. D. 130, and it continued in alliance with them nearly one hundred and fifty years.   Its magnificence and prosperity under the government of its queen, Zenobia, and its utter subversion by the emperor Aurelian (who took her prisoner), A. D. 275, are related by the Roman historians.   Its advantageous position soon restored its prosperity : it was, however, sacked a second time by the Saracens, when they triumphed in the East, after which this once celebrated seat of commerce and the arts gradually sunk into an obscure town and a trifling fortress.

The present population of Palmyra is estimated by Mr. Burckhardt at about one thousand inhabitants.   Its splendid remains were first visited by some English merchants from Aleppo, in 1691 : and in 1751 Messrs.

Dawkins and Wood, two English gentlemen, measured and delineated all the principal buildings of this once celebrated city, with singular fidelity and ability.

It is scarcely possible to conceive any thing more magnificent than the view of the ruins of Palmyra, when they burst upon the eye, as seen from the Valley of the Tombs. In the space covered by these ruins, we sometimes find a palace, of which nothing remains but the court and walls; sometimes a temple, the peristyle of which is half thrown down; and now a portico, a gallery, or a triumphal arch. If, from this striking scene, we cast our eyes upon the ground, another view, almost as varied, presents itself. On which side soever we look, the earth is strewed with vast stones, half-buried, with broken entablatures, mutilated friezes, disfigured reliefs, effaced sculptures, violated tombs, and altars defiled by the dust. Our view exhibits part of the ruined city of Palmyra, taken from the north-east. On the summit of the eminence on the right is a large castle, erected, according to tradition, by one of the Emirs of the Druses: it commands a view to the westward as far as the peaks of Mount Lebanon, and to the eastward are the whole extent of the ruins, and the boundless desert beyond. The foreground is occupied by splendid columns, with their entablatures, not yet destroyed by the consuming hand of time. The group of figures in the centre will convey an idea of the oriental mode of travelling. The more distinguished ruin is the great Temple of the Sun, with its court and portico; which, when perfect, must have been a magnificent building: but the other remains are remarkable rather for their number than for their grandeur. Of the remains without the walls of the antient city, the most distinguished are the tombs erected on the sides of the defile in the mountain through which Tadmor is approached from the west: they are lofty towers, divided into five stories, each of the chambers being about twelve feet by eight, and containing five or six tiers of repositories for bodies. The inhabitants derive their revenue partly from the manufacture of salt, of which there are some large pits near the town, and partly from the vegetable alkali which they prepare from the kelp of the desert.

₊ Fuller's Tour through some Parts of the Turkish Empire, pp. 438—442.; Irby and Mangles's Travels, pp. 267—273. But, for minute details respecting these remains of antient architecture, the reader is necessarily referred to Mr. Wood's splendid work on " The Ruins of Palmyra," published at London in 1753, in folio, which was reprinted with impressions from the original plates in 1827.

Drawn by D. Roberts, from a sketch by Mrs Bracebridge.

Engraved by E. Finden.

SAMARIA.

I. KINGS, XIII. 32.

SAMARIA.

Drawn by D. Roberts, from a Sketch by Mrs. Bracebridge and
M. Léon de Laborde.

SAMARIA was a celebrated city, situated near the middle of Palestine:
it was built by Omri, king of Israel, on a hill of the same name
(1 Kings, xvi. 18. 24.), and became the metropolis of the kingdom of
Israel, that is, of the ten tribes, as Jerusalem was the capital of the
kingdom of Judah. It was taken by Shalmaneser king of Assyria, after
a siege of three years (2 Kings, xviii. 9, 10.); it was rebuilt by the
inhabitants whom he left in the land, and was again destroyed by John
Hyrcanus. The Roman proconsul Gabinius once more restored it, and
called it Gabinia; and it was afterwards given by the emperor Augustus
to Herod, misnamed the Great, who enlarged and adorned it, and increased its population by introducing sixteen thousand emigrants. Dr.
Richardson, in 1818, observed numerous columns and other remains of
various edifices, which attest its antient splendour: among these structures erected by Herod was a temple, in honour of Augustus Cæsar,
from which the city obtained the Greek name ΣΕΒΑΣΤΗ (*Sebasté*),
corresponding with the Latin Augusta. Samaria was between forty and
fifty miles distant from Jerusalem. In February, 1833, when the Hon.
Capt. Fitzmaurice visited this place, the solitary tower represented in
our engraving marked the spot where antient Sebasté once stood. It
is a remnant of one of those numerous churches built by the empress
Helena, to transmit to posterity the sites of the old Israelitish cities.
" But here, as in every thing else connected with this unhappy country,
time and desolation have completed that destruction, which the hand of
the spoiler has left unfinished; and the screams of the vulture and the
howlings of the jackal are the only sounds that now issue from the spot,
whence the smoke of incense was wont to ascend at the evening sacrifice, and the praises of the Almighty rose from the lips of his chosen
people."

The church, which is completely a ruin, is built of grey stone; and
the arches of the windows are supported on a cluster of slight columns.
The edifice rises from a precipitous bank of rocky limestone, at the
bottom of which is a broken wall. Close to the wall of the church

Pt. 23.

grow masses of the *Cactus Opuntia*, and a single aloe-tree. The path which leads round the crown of the hill to the church is a steep ascent, rocky, and incumbered with stones which have fallen down from the wall. The trees seen in our view are olives, of great antiquity, and of luxuriant growth; the stems of which are knarled and twisted very fantastically. The foreground is very rocky and broken, with a little short grass appearing here and there under the trees.

Modern Samaria is a small and poor village, steep of approach, but strong by nature, and beautifully situated. It stands on a fine large insulated hill, encompassed by a broad, deep valley, which is surrounded by four hills, one on each side: these are cultivated in terraces to the top, sown with grain, and planted (as the valley also is) with fig and olive trees.

₊ Dr. Richardson's Travels, vol. ii. pp. 412, 413. The Hon. Capt. W. E. Fitzmaurice's (unpublished) Cruise to Egypt, &c. pp. 55, 56. MS. Communication from Mrs. Bracebridge.

Drawn by A.W. Callcott, R.A. from a sketch by the Revd R. Master.

Engraved by E. Finden.

VIEW FROM MOUNT CARMEL,

with Ptolemais Acre in the Distance.

1 KINGS XVIII. 42.

VIEW FROM MOUNT CARMEL,

PTOLEMAIS (ACRE) IN THE DISTANCE.

Drawn by A. W. Callcott, from a Sketch made on the Spot by the Rev. R. Master.

Mount Carmel is a range of very rocky hills, extending six or eight miles nearly north and south, and terminating in the promontory or cape which forms the bay of Accho, or Acre, and from the summit of which our view is taken. The city of Acre is seen in the distance. Carmel is computed to be between fifteen hundred and two thousand feet above the level of the sea, which washes its base. Altogether it forms one of the most grand and striking promontories, which occur along the shores of the Mediterranean. At its foot runs the river Kishon. The sides of this now barren and desolate ridge are graced by some native cedars and brambles, still intermingled with wild vines and olives, which denote its antient fertility or more careful cultivation : but there are no longer any rich pastures, to render it the habitation of shepherds, or to recal to the fancy the beauty of Carmel and of Sharon, and to justify the comparison of it to the glory of Libanus. There are many caves in this mountainous range, particularly on the western side, the largest of which, called the School of Elijah, is much venerated both by Jews and Mohammedans. On the summit, facing the sea, tradition says that the Prophet stood, when he prayed for rain, and beheld the cloud arise out of the sea: but the great object here, which attracts the religious traveller, is a cave, believed to be that in which Elijah concealed himself from the persecution of Ahab and Jezebel (1 Kings xix. 9.), after his triumph over the idolatrous priests of Baal, four hundred and fifty of whom he had commanded to be put to death. (1 Kings xviii. 19—40.)

The monastery which stands on the summit of the mountainous ridge, near the spot where the Prophet offered up his sacrifice, was long the residence of the Carmelite friars. It appears never to have been a fine building, and it is now entirely abandoned. During the campaign of the French in Syria, it was converted into an hospital for the sick, for which it was well adapted by its healthy and retired situation. It was afterwards ravaged by the Turks, who stripped its shrines, and destroyed its roof; though there still remains, for the solace of devout visitors, a small stone altar in a grotto dedicated to Saint Elias, over which is a coarse painting representing the Prophet leaning on a wheel, with fire and other instruments of sacrifice at his side.

*** Carne's Letters from the East, p. 249.; Buckingham's Travels in Palestine, pp. 119, 120.; Rae Wilson's Travels, vol. ii. pp. 50—54.

Pt. 4.

FOUNTAIN AT JERICHO, (JUDEA.)

Called the Fountain of Elisha.

2 KINGS II. 19-22.

Drawing A.W. Gilbert R.A. from a sketch by the Rev.d R. Masters.

Engraved by W Finden.

FOUNTAIN AT JERICHO;

CALLED THE FOUNTAIN OF ELISHA.

Drawn by A. W. CALLCOTT, from a Sketch by the Rev. R. MASTER, M. A.

THE country or plain around Jericho was one of the most fertile spots in Palestine, abounding in palm trees (whence it is called the "city of palm trees" in Deut. xxxiv. 3.), and yielding also great quantities of the opo-balsamum (balsam or balm of Gilead), so highly esteemed in Oriental courts, even to the present day.

On entering the mountains which protect the western side of the plain of Jericho, the attention of the traveller is invited to the FOUNTAIN OF ELISHA, the waters of which were sweetened by a miracle performed by that prophet. The men of Jericho having represented to him that, though the situation of the town was pleasant, " the water was naught, and the ground barren," Elisha " said, Bring me a new cruse, and put salt therein. And they brought it to him. And he went forth unto the spring of the waters, and cast the salt in there, and said, Thus saith the LORD, I have healed these waters; there shall not be from thence any more death or barren land. So the waters were healed unto this day, according to the saying of Elisha which he spake." (2 Kings, ii. 19—22.)

The waters of the Fountain of Elisha are at present received in a basin, about nine or ten paces long, and five or six broad; whence, issuing out in a copious stream, they divide themselves into several small streams, dispersing their refreshment to the land as far as Jericho, and rendering it exceedingly fruitful. Noble trees grow close by this fountain, the spreading boughs of which afford a grateful shade to the traveller.

*** Maundrell's Journey from Aleppo, p. 108. Buckingham's Travels in Palestine, pp. 292, 293. Sir F. Henniker's Notes during a Visit to Egypt, Nubia, &c. pp. 289—291. Russell's Palestine, pp. 254. 259.

JAFFA — JOPPA.

JOPPA.

Drawn by J. M. W. TURNER, from a Sketch made on the spot by the Rev. R. M. MASTER.

JOPPA, by the Arabs called Jaffa, is the chief sea-port of Palestine: at the division of the country it fell to the lot of the tribe of Dan. (Josh. xix. 46.) The timber hewn upon Mount Lebanon for Solomon was floated to this port. (2 Chron. ii. 16.) Here the prophet Jonah embarked for Tarshish. (Jon. i. 3.) Here also Peter raised Tabitha from the dead (Acts ix. 36—42.); and, while he was in the house of Simon a tanner, he saw an emblematical vision, indicating that the gospel should be preached not only to the Jews but also to the Gentiles. (Acts x. 9. xi. 1.) The dwelling of the British vice-consul (Signor Damiani), in 1831, stood on the reputed site of this house; and a portion of antient wall therein was pointed out as a genuine relic of the original mansion. During the war of the Jews with the Romans Joppa was burnt, but was soon rebuilt. Afterwards, however, it became the strong-hold of pirates, who infested the neighbouring seas, in consequence of which it was utterly destroyed. It was again rebuilt in the time of the crusades, and soon became a flourishing place, as being the only good harbour on the coast of Palestine.

Modern Jaffa stands upon a conical hill or promontory, the base of which on three sides is washed by the sea: as a station for vessels, its harbour is one of the worst in the Mediterranean; and ships generally anchor about a mile from the town, in order to avoid the shoals and rocks of the place. Towards the land the town is defended by a wall: it contains no very remarkable buildings, and the streets are narrow, irregular, and ill paved, as is the case with all oriental towns. The hospital, where Buonaparte poisoned his sick soldiers on his retreat, in order to prevent them from falling into the hands of the Turks, is now the Armenian convent: one of the priests, who was in the town at the time, informed Captains Irby and Mangles that there were *only* thirty-five men thus poisoned. On the beach, about a mile to the south-west of the town, Buonaparte inhumanly massacred four thousand men in cold blood, after they had surrendered upon promise of quarter. They were Barbaresques, (natives of Algiers, Tunis, and other towns on the Barbary coast,) who had been sent to the assistance of Djezzar Pasha. Buonaparte's plea for putting them to death was, that they had previously been prisoners, who had been liberated upon their parole, which they had broken.

The inhabitants of Jaffa are stated to be four or five thousand in number, of whom about six hundred are Christians, of the Romish, Greek, and Armenian communions: of the Christian portion of the population the Greeks are described as being by far the most affable and agreeable to strangers. The water-melons, which are produced in the gardens of Jaffa, are celebrated all over the Levant for their delicious flavour.

** Dr. Clarke's Travels, vol. iv. p. 442. Irby's and Mangles' Travels, pp. 186—188. Dr. Richardson's Travels, vol. ii. pp. 208. 215, 216. Three Weeks in Palestine, pp. 6. 9, 10.

75

Drawn by D. Roberts, from a sketch by F. Catherwood.

Engraved by E. Finden.

JERUSALEM. — THE MOSQUE OF OMAR.

On Mount Moriah, where the Temple of Solomon stood.

I KINGS VI. II CHRON. III. 2.

JERUSALEM.

PULPIT IN THE MOSQUE OF OMAR;

WHICH EDIFICE IS ERECTED ON MOUNT MORIAH, ON THE SITE OF SOLOMON'S TEMPLE.

Drawn by S. PROUT, from a Sketch made on the spot by F. CATHERWOOD, Esq.

THE prophet Jeremiah, foretelling the desolation of Jerusalem and the abandonment of the ungrateful and disobedient Israelites by the Almighty, introduces the Deity as saying, " I have forsaken mine house," meaning the temple (Jer. xii. 7.). This declaration unquestionably referred to the desolation made by the Babylonians, when Jerusalem was sacked by Nebuchadnezzar. It may however be applied in a wider sense to the Almighty finally forsaking the place, where he had declared that he would " put his name." Literally, indeed, may it be affirmed that God has " forsaken his house," since Mount Moriah (2 Chron. iii. 1.), on which was erected the magnificent temple of Solomon, is now covered by the mosque of Omar, in which the followers of the pseudo-prophet of Arabia offer their devotions.

As a view and description of this edifice will appear in a succeeding part of this work, the reader's attention is now invited to the truly splendid PULPIT delineated in the accompanying engraving. It is situated on the highest platform of the mosque, and nearly opposite to its southern gate, called the Gate of Prayer. The material of which it is composed is of white marble, with the exception of the small columns, which are of verde antique, rosso antico, &c. From whatever point it is viewed, it has a picturesque appearance; and it is of the usual form of the pulpits found in the Mohammedan mosques. The enterprising artist, by whom it was sketched, was the first European who was ever permitted to make a drawing in this mosque, which in the estimation of the Moslems is inferior in point of sanctity only to the Caaba at Mecca. It should seem that this pulpit is but rarely used for the purpose of preaching; as, during nearly two months of daily visits to the mosque of Omar, Mr. Catherwood never once heard the Imam preach from it; — a small pulpit in the interior of that building being used for that purpose. It is probably of equal antiquity with the mosque itself, though Mr. C. observed no date by which its age could be determined.

₊ Manuscript Communication from F. Catherwood, Esq.

Drawn by J.D. Harding from a sketch by Las Casas.

Engraved by W. Finden

SEPULCHRES OF THE SONS OF DAVID.

(commonly called the Tombs of the Kings, near Jerusalem.)

2 CHRON XXXII 33

SEPULCHRES OF THE SONS OF DAVID,

COMMONLY CALLED

THE TOMBS OF THE KINGS, NEAR JERUSALEM.

Drawn by J. D. HARDING, from a View by M. DE CASAS.

NEARLY a mile from Jerusalem, on the north, lie the Tombs of the Kings as they are commonly termed, though it is difficult to account for this appellation being given to them; for it is certain that none either of the kings of Israel or Judah were buried here, as the Scriptures assign other places for their sepulchres; unless, perhaps, Hezekiah was here interred, and these were the "sepulchres of the sons of David" mentioned in 2 Chron. xxxii. 33. Whoever was buried here, it is certain that the place itself discovers so great an expense both of labour and treasure, that we may well suppose it to have been the work of kings. The approach to these sepulchres is through a passage cut in the rock into an open square having the appearance of a quarry, whose western side was quite smooth and perpendicular, in which is excavated a porch of about ten yards in length by four in depth. Over this porch are carved festoons of fruits and flowers, very beautifully executed, exhibiting an advanced stage of art, though now very much defaced. On the left is the entrance into the sepulchral chambers, so filled with rubbish, that the traveller is obliged to lie down, and creep in like a lizard, to gain admittance. Through this he is conducted into a square chamber, having three doorways, on three different sides, leading to other chambers (in all, six or seven in number), cut with mathematical exactness, the walls being perfectly smooth. In these were hewn recesses, of different shapes, for the reception of bodies, some being oblong, and others the segment of a circle. In one of these apartments was a row of smaller niches, in size and form resembling the *columbaria* of the Romans, and in the floor are sunk quadrangular receptacles of the size of a coffin. Strewed about, are fragments of sarcophagi, covered with carvings of fruit, flowers, and foliage, similar to that which ornamented the frieze of the portico.

Maundrell states, that he found one of the doors still upon its hinges: such is not now the case. But the intelligent author of "Three Weeks in Palestine" (who concurs in Maundrell's opinion that these tombs were the

Pt. 16.

sepulchre of Helena, queen of Adiabene, and her family), states that he " saw one door still perfect, and very singular and beautiful it was, hewn out of the same compact limestone which forms the rock, half a foot in thickness: the pannels were as nicely cut as the finest mahogany doors in this country, and the whole highly polished. It had originally turned upon tenons of one piece with itself, resting on sockets in the solid rock; so that no extraneous matter was used for hinges, fitting most exactly in the door-frame, shutting apparently with its own weight, and requiring pressure to push it open. There was no sign of bolt or fastening of any kind about it. In several of these crypts were fragments of similar doors."

*** Maundrell's Journey from Aleppo to Jerusalem, pp. 102—104. Carne's Letters from the East, p. 294. Three Weeks in Palestine, pp. 74—77.

THE SUMMIT OF MOUNT TABOR.

PSALM LXXXIX. 12.

THE SUMMIT OF MOUNT TABOR.

Drawn by the Hon. Capt. W. E. FITZMAURICE.

MOUNT TABOR, by the Arabs called Djebel Tour, is situated in the middle of Galilee, on the confines of the allotment of the tribes of Issachar and Naphtali: it is comprehended in the portion assigned to the children of Issachar, as their inheritance in the land of Canaan (Josh. xix. 17—23.), and is one of those elevations where Jesus Christ was accustomed to retire for meditation and prayer. In the Old Testament it is classed with Mount Hermon (Psalm lxxxix. 12.), which is distinctly seen from it. Referring the reader to Part X., in which another view and description of this mountain are given, together with the diversified and extensive scenery which it commands, we now invite his attention to a few particulars more immediately connected with its summit.

This conical mountain is computed to be about a mile in height, and its summit is flat and very fertile, being thickly studded with trees and shrubs; though towards the south it is more open; and from that quarter there is a most delightful view, which abundantly compensates for the exertion attending the difficult ascent up its rugged and precipitous sides. Antiently, it would seem that a city was built upon this summit, and assigned with its suburbs to the children of Merari. (1 Chron. vi. 77.) To the west are scattered fragments of walls and other ruins. The empress Helena founded here two monasteries, one in memory of Moses, and the other of Elias. The Hon. Capt. Fitzmaurice saw here, in February, 1833, the ruins of a very antient church, built over the spot where the Transfiguration is supposed to have taken place. Three grottos or excavations in the rock, by the neighbouring monks called " Tria Tabernacula," were pointed out to Mr. Rae Wilson, as having been made to commemorate that event; the remembrance of which is perpetuated by an annual procession to a rude altar, at which various acts of devotion are performed.

⁎ Hon. Capt. Fitzmaurice's (unpublished) Cruise to Egypt. &c. p. 56. Rae Wilson's Travels, vol. ii. pp. 32—36. Madox's Excursions in the Holy Land, &c. vol. ii. p. 250.

Drawn by A.N. Callcott R. A. from a sketch by Albert Way Esq.

VIEW FROM MOUNT LEBANON.

Looking down the Valley of the Nahr el Kelb River

Engraved by E. Finden.

VIEW FROM THE RANGE OF LEBANON,

LOOKING DOWN

THE VALLEY OF NAHR EL KELB.

Drawn by A. W. CALLCOTT, from a Sketch made on the spot by ALBERT WAY, Esq.

.... " a well of living waters, and streams from Lebanon." — *Sol. Song*, iv. 15.

THIS view of the mountainous range of Lebanon is taken a few miles to the north of Beyroot or Berytus. An antient road passes over a part of it; which, in an inscription seen by Dr. Pococke, is called the Via Antoniniana, from the emperor Aurelius Antoninus, by whose command it was made. Through the valley below this road runs the NAHR EL KELB, as it is called in Arabic; it is the Lycus of the Greeks, that is, the Dog River, so termed from the statue of a dog which was formerly there. On one side of the road Dr. Pococke (who travelled early in the eighteenth century) saw a ruin something like the pedestal of a statue; and below it in the sea, at the mouth of the river, was a large stone which was exhibited as the statue of a dog. The same traveller also observed a relief cut in the rock, which seemed to have represented a dog. Antiently, the Lycus or Nahr el Kelb was navigable, notwithstanding the rapidity of the stream. Mr. Madox, who visited this part of Lebanon in August, 1824, found the banks of the Dog River covered with plantations of mulberry trees, and the mountains covered with pine trees.

*** Pococke's Description of the East, vol. ii. p. 92. Madox's Excursions in the Holy Land, &c., vol. ii. p. 57.

34.

SOLOMON'S POOLS.

Drawn by J.M.W.Turner, R.A from a sketch by C.Barry Esq.

Engraved by J. Stephenson

SOLOMON'S POOLS.

Drawn by J. M. W. Turner, from a Sketch made on the spot by Charles Barry, Esq.

The Pools of Solomon are situated about one hour's distance to the south of Bethlehem; and to them the King of Israel is supposed to refer in Eccles. ii. 4—6., where, among other magnificent works executed by him, he enumerates vineyards, gardens, orchards, and pools. These pools are three in number, of an oblong quadrangular form, cut out of the native rock, and are covered with a thick coat of plaster in the inside, and supported by abutments: the workmanship throughout, like every thing Jewish, is more remarkable for strength than beauty. They are situated in a most secluded situation, at the south end of a small valley, in the midst of mountains; and are so disposed on the sloping hill, that the water in the uppermost pool flows into the second, and thence into the third. That on the west is nearest to the source of the spring which supplies it with water, and is stated by Dr. Richardson to be 480 feet long; the second is about 600 feet, and the third about 660 feet in length. The breadth of them all is nearly the same: but no traveller, antient or modern, has ascertained their depth. The pools communicate freely with each other; and are capable of containing a great quantity of water, which they discharge into a small aqueduct that conveys it to Jerusalem. This aqueduct was constructed all along on the surface of the ground, and framed of perforated stones let one into another, with a fillet round the cavity, so framed as to prevent leakage; and united to each other with so firm a cement, that they will sometimes sooner break than endure a separation. These pipes were covered, for greater security, with a case or layer of smaller stones, which were laid over them in a very strong mortar. "The whole work," says Maundrell, "seems to be endued with such absolute firmness, as if it had been designed for eternity. But the Turks have demonstrated, in this instance, that nothing can be so well wrought but they are able to destroy it. For of this strong aqueduct, which was carried formerly five or six leagues with so vast expense and labour, you now see only here and there a fragment remaining."

The fountain, whence these pools principally derive their waters, is at

Pt. 8.

the distance of about 140 paces from them. This, the friars of Bethlehem are fully persuaded, is the "sealed fountain" to which Solomon
compares his bride. (Sol. Song. iv. 12.) In confirmation of their
opinion, they pretend a tradition, that King Solomon shut up these
springs, and kept the door of them sealed with his signet, in order that
he might preserve the waters for his drinking in their natural freshness
and purity. Nor was it difficult thus to secure them, as they rise under
ground, and there is no avenue to them but by a little hole, like the
mouth of a narrow well. Through this hole you descend directly,
though not without some difficulty, for about four yards, when you arrive
in a vaulted room, forty-five feet in length and twenty-four in breadth;
adjoining to which there is another room of the same kind, but somewhat less. Both these rooms are covered with handsome stone arches,
of great antiquity, which Maundrell thinks may be the work of Solomon.

Below these pools, at the distance of more than half a mile, is a deep
valley, enclosed on each side by lofty mountains, which the monks of
Bethlehem affirm to be the "enclosed garden" alluded to in Sol. Song,
iv. 12. Whether this conjecture (for it is no more than a conjecture)
be well founded or not, Maundrell thinks it probable enough that the
pools may be the same with Solomon's; there not being the like supply
of excellent spring water to be met with any where else throughout
Palestine. But if Solomon made the gardens in the rocky ground now
assigned for them, it may be safely affirmed, that he demonstrated
greater power and wealth in finishing his design than he did wisdom in
selecting the place for it.

₊ Maundrell's Travels, pp. 118—122. Dr. Richardson's Travels, vol. ii. pp. 379,
380. Rae Wilson's Travels, vol. i. pp. 267—269.

Drawn by C. Stanfield R. A. from a sketch by F. Catherwood.

Engraved by W. Finden.

E G Y P T.

The Temple and broken Statue of Memnon, Thebes

"The Idols of Egypt shall be moved."   ISA xix 1

EGYPT.

TEMPLE AND BROKEN STATUE OF MEMNON,

IN THE MEMNONIUM, OR PALACE AND TEMPLE OF RAMESES II., SURNAMED MIAMUN.

Drawn by C. STANFIELD, A.R.A., from a Sketch made on the spot by
F. CATHERWOOD, Esq.

THE term MEMNONIUM is used by the Greek geographer Strabo to designate that part of antient Thebes which lies on the west side of the river. The French savans (and after them some modern travellers) have, without any sufficient reason, restricted it to the magnificent ruin delineated in our engraving, which may be regarded as a literal fulfilment of the prophetic denunciation in Isa. xix. 1., " The idols of Egypt shall be moved at his presence." This edifice is the palace and temple of Rameses II. king of Egypt, surnamed Miamun, which title was probably corrupted by the Romans into Memnon, and became the origin of the word Memnonium. It stands on the western side of the river Nile, on the edge of the cultivated plain: and from its very great strength, having but few exterior openings, it is not improbable that the Memnonium was used as a fortress.

For symmetry and elegance of sculpture, this building may vie with any other monument of Egyptian art. It is confessedly one of the finest remains of antiquity at Thebes. " No traces," (says Mr. Wilkinson, whose enterprising researches have first made fully known the nature of the Memnonium,) " are visible of the dromos*, that probably existed before the pyramidal towers which form the façade of the first hypæthral area, a court whose breadth of one hundred and eighty feet is reduced to a more just proportion, by the introduction of a double avenue of columns on either side, extending from the towers to the north wall." The figures standing upright, with their backs to the piers, formed part of this court yard: they probably are not less than twenty-five feet in height. In this area, on the right of a flight of steps, was the stupendous statue of the king, of syenite, or rose-coloured granite from the quarries in the neighbourhood of Assouan or Syene: it was seated on a throne,

---

* The dromos was a paved approach to Egyptian temples, generally formed by an avenue of sphinxes: sometimes two statues, or stellæ, commenced the avenue.

in the usual attitude of these Egyptian figures, the hand resting on his knees, indicative of that tranquillity which he had returned to enjoy in Egypt, after the fatigues of victory. But the fury of an invader has levelled this monument of Egyptian grandeur, whose colossal fragments are seen in our engraving, lying scattered around the pedestal, and its shivered throne evinces the force used for its demolition. The features of the face are no longer discernible. " The throne and legs are completely destroyed, and reduced to comparatively small fragments; while the upper part, broken at the waist, is merely thrown back upon the ground, and lies in that position, which was the consequence of its fall; nor are there any marks of the wedge or other instrument which should have been employed for reducing those fragments to the state in which they now appear. The fissures seen across the head, and in the pedestal, are the work of a later period, when some of these blocks were cut for millstones by the Arabs; but its previous overthrow will probably be coëval with the Persian invasion. To say that this is the largest statue in Egypt, will convey no idea of the size or enormous weight of a mass, which, from an approximate calculation, exceeded, when entire, nearly three times the great obelisk of Karnak [a], and weighed about eight hundred and eighty-seven tons, five hundred weight and a half." (Mr. Catherwood calculates its weight at little short of one thousand tons.) This is, in fact, the largest detached statue in the world: and it is justly a source of wonder among all well-informed engineers, how such enormous masses could have been worked and fixed, since it is all but certain that iron was unknown at the period when this statue was executed. The small head half buried in the earth, to the left of the picture, is of the same size as that in the British Museum, which has been so justly admired for the noble expression of its countenance. The back-ground in our view represents cultivated land.

[a] This obelisk weighs about two hundred and ninety-seven tons, ten hundred weight, and two thirds, allowing two thousand three hundred and sixty ounces to a cubic foot.

₊ Wilkinson's Topography of Thebes, &c. pp. 9—12. 39. Manuscript Communication from F. Catherwood, Esq.

Drawn by J. D. Harding, from a Sketch by C. Barry, Esq.

THE CEDARS OF LEBANON.

Engraved by W. Finden.

THE CEDARS OF LEBANON.

Drawn by J. D. HARDING, from a Sketch made on the spot by CHARLES BARRY, Esq.

THE mountainous range of Lebanon, of which a view and general description have been given in Part III., was celebrated for the extent of its forests, and particularly for the size and excellency of its cedars. The ascent from the village of Eden, or Aden, near Tripoli, to the spot where the cedars grow, is inconsiderable. This distance is computed by Captains Irby and Mangles to be about five miles, allowing for the windings of the road, which is very rugged, and passes over hill and dale. These far-famed trees are situated on a small eminence in a valley at the foot of the highest part of the mountain : the land on the mountain's side has a sterile aspect, and the trees are remarkable by being altogether in one clump. By the natives they are called Arsilebàn. There are, in fact, two generations of trees : the oldest are large and massy, four, five, or even seven trunks springing from one base ; they rear their heads to an enormous height, spreading their branches afar ; and they are not found in any other part of Lebanon, though young trees are occasionally met with.

The antient cedars — those which superstition has consecrated as holy, and which are the chief object of the traveller's curiosity, have been gradually diminishing in number for the last three centuries. In 1550, Belloni found them to be twenty-eight in number ; Rauwolf, in 1575, counted twenty-four ; Dandini in 1600, and Thevenot about fifty years after, enumerated twenty-three ; which Maundrell, in 1697, states were reduced to sixteen. Dr. Pococke, in 1738, found fifteen standing, and one which had been recently blown down. Burckhardt, in 1810, counted eleven or twelve ; twenty-five others were very large ones, about fifty of middling size, and more than three hundred smaller and young ones. Lastly, in 1818, Dr. Richardson found that the old cedars, " the glory of Lebanon," were no more than seven in number. In the course of another century, it is probable that not a vestige of them will remain, and the predictions of the prophets will then be most literally fulfilled : — " Lebanon is ashamed and hewn down. The high ones of stature shall be hewn down : Lebanon shall fall mightily." (Isa. xxxiii. 9. x. 33, 34.) " Upon the mountains and in all the vallies his branches are fallen ; to the end that none of all the trees by the water exalt themselves for their height,

Pt. 13.

neither shoot up their top among the thick boughs." (Ezek. xxxi. 12. 14.) "Open thy doors, O Lebanon, that the fire may destroy thy cedars. The cedar is fallen ; the forest of the vintage is come down." (Zech. xi. 1, 2.)

The trunks of the old trees are covered with the names of travellers, and other persons who have visited them, some of which go as far back as 1640. These trunks are described by Burckhardt as seeming to be quite dead ; their wood is of a grey tint. Maundrell, in 1697, measured one, which he found to be twelve yards and six inches in girth, and thirty-seven yards in the spread of its boughs : at above five or six yards from the ground it was divided into five limbs, each of which was equal to a great tree. Forty-one years afterwards, (viz. in 1738,) Dr. Pococke measured one which had the roundest body, though not the largest, and found it twenty-four feet in circumference ; another, with a sort of triple body and of a triangular figure, measured twelve feet on each side. In 1818, Dr. Richardson measured one, which he afterwards discovered was not the largest in the clump, and found it to be thirty-two feet in circumference. Finally, in 1824, Mr. Madox rested under the branches of a cedar, which measured twenty-seven feet in circumference, a little way from the ground : after which he measured the largest of the trees now standing, which he found to be thirty-nine or forty feet in circumference : it has three very large stems, and seven large branches, with various smaller ones.

The cedars of Lebanon are frequently mentioned in the sacred writings. Besides their uncommon size and beauty of shape and foliage, (which must be borne in mind in order to enter fully into the meaning of the sacred writers,) they send forth a fragrant odour, which seems to be intended by " the smell of Lebanon." (Hos. xiv. 6. Sol. Song, iv. 11.) Its timber was used in the erection of the first and second temple at Jerusalem, as well as of the palace of Solomon ; and in the last-mentioned edifice, so much cedar-wood appears to have been used, that it was called " the house of the forest of Lebanon." (1 Kings vii. 2. x. 19.) The Tyrians used it in ship-building (Ezek. xxvii. 5, 6.)

₊ Maundrell's Travels, p. 191. Pococke's Description of the East, book ii. chap. v. Burckhardt's Travels in Syria, p. 19. Dr. Richardson's Travels, vol. ii. pp. 512, 513. Captains Irby's and Mangles' Travels, pp. 209, 210. Modern Traveller, vol. ii. p. 136. Rae Wilson's Travels, vol. ii. pp. 104—106. Madox's Excursions in the Holy Land, &c. vol. ii. p. 103.

THE RANGE OF LEBANON.

From Bairout.

Drawn by C. Stanfield, A.R.A. from a sketch by the Honble W. E. Fitzmaurice.

Engraved by W. Finden.

THE RANGE OF LEBANON FROM BAIROUT.

Drawn by C. STANFIELD, from a Sketch made on the spot by the
Hon. W. E. FITZMAURICE.

THE mighty Lebanon, the natural phenomena of which have been described in a former part of this work, is here exhibited in a different point of view. Its rugged peaks afford very extensive prospects over the surrounding country. As this mountainous range and Mount Carmel formed the principal parts of the dominions of Hezekiah, king of Judah, the Assyrian monarch Sennacherib, flushed with victory and success, thus alludes to them in his menacing message to the Jewish king:—" By the multitude of my chariots am I come up to the height of the mountains, to the SIDES OF LEBANON; and I will cut down the tall cedars thereof; and the choice fir trees thereof: and I will enter into the height of his border, and the forest of his Carmel." (Isa. xxxviii. 24. 2 Kings xix. 23.) The import of which proud vaunt is, that Sennacherib would take possession of all the strong holds, as well as the most fruitful places of the country, by making an entire conquest of it.

Our view is taken from BAIROUT, or Bayreuth (the antient Berytus), which stands on a gentle rising ground close by the sea-shore. The town, which is inclosed with walls, encircles a small bay, which is defended at one extremity by a castle erected on a promontory, and bearing a close resemblance to the remains of feudal castles, which are occasionally to be seen in England. Bairout is supplied with fresh water by several rivulets that fall from the neighbouring hills. It was taken from the Saracens by Baldwin I., king of Jerusalem, in 1111, and retaken in 1187; ten years afterwards the Christians recaptured it, and it was frequently ravaged during the crusades. At this period it was a large fortified town, and a depôt for the costly merchandise of Damascus. Subsequently, it fell into the hands of the Druses, from whom it was taken by the Turks, who still retain possession of it. The pier belonging to the harbour of Bairout is constructed entirely of fragments of marble columns, relics of the antient Berytus. The surrounding country is rich and highly cultivated, being covered with fruit-trees and white mulberry-trees for the growth of silk, which is its staple production. Behind the whole majestically rises the mighty Lebanon.

The Druses, who reside in the mountains not far from Bairout, are a martial and independent tribe, who are under the command of one chief-

Pt. 5.

tain: their number has been calculated at about one hundred thousand persons, and their language is pure Arabic. They keep close together about Lebanon, in all probability after the manner of the antient Jews, who considered it unlawful to associate with those of another nation. No Mohammedan is permitted to reside in their district. They frequently come to Bairout to purchase such commodities as they want; and Druses may frequently be seen walking in the streets of the town.

Of the peculiar tenets of this extraordinary race little is known, as they are rigidly kept secret among themselves. They are divided into two classes: viz. 1. The uninitiated, who comprehend the far greater number, and who are very imperfectly acquainted with the tenets of their own sect; and, 2. The Akkals, or initiated, who are admitted to their private assemblies only after a certain probation, and who alone are fully instructed in the articles of their belief, whatever they may be. The image of a calf is said to be the object of their adoration. Externally, they profess the religion of the strongest, and in Syria they conform to Mohammedism, attending the mosques and keeping the Turkish fast of Ramadan; but they transgress without scruple the laws of the pseudo-prophet of Arabia, whenever they can do so unobserved. They evince the utmost hatred for all religions except their own, and intermarry only among themselves. The union of brothers and sisters is permitted: they have only one wife at a time, but they divorce her upon the slightest pretext. Their character is profligate and perfidious; but the laws of hospitality are held so sacred, that they have never been known to betray any who took refuge among them. In the dress of the females many are distinguished by a *tantoura*, or large horn of silver, or of copper silvered over, according to the opulence of the wearer: it is a foot and a half or two feet in length, springing from the top of the forehead like the horn of the fabled unicorn, and is adorned with figures of stars, animals, and a variety of patterns. Over this hangs a scarf or shawl, by means of which the wearer can conceal her features at pleasure. This custom is supposed to have been derived from the Hebrews; among whom the horn was symbolical of power, and has given rise to numerous allusions in the Scriptures. See 1 Kings xxii. 11. 2 Chron. xviii. 10. Psalm xviii. 2. lxxv. 4, 5. 10. Dan. vii. 24. Micah iv. 13. Zech. i. 21. and Rev. xvii. 12.

₂ Irby's and Mangles' Travels, pp. 202, 203. Madden's Excursions in the Holy Land, &c. vol. ii. pp. 89, 90. Wilson's Travels in the Holy Land, &c. vol. ii. pp. 163 —165. Three Weeks in Palestine, pp. 101—107. 134.

Drawn from a sketch by C. Barry Esq.

Engraved by E. Finden.

EGYPT.

The Ruined Temples at Philæ.

"The Idols of Egypt shall be moved." ISAIAH XIX 1

EGYPT.

RUINED TEMPLES AT PHILÆ.

Drawn by D. Roberts, from a Sketch made on the spot by C. Barry, Esq.

Philæ is an island in the river Nile, above the first cataract; it is situated in latitude 24° 1′ 28″ N., and in longitude 32° 54′ 16″ E. The learned geographer, Bochart, is of opinion, that this island is the place designated as Phul (or Pul) in Isa. lxvi. 19.; the prophet (or, more probably, some subsequent copyist) having written פּוּל [PHUL] for פּיל [PHIL], by a permutation of the Hebrew letters vau and yod, which is of very frequent occurrence in Hebrew manuscripts. Phul, therefore, must mean the Egyptians in the passage just cited. Philæ is the eastern-most of a group of islands and rocks, which compose the first cataract; it is about one thousand feet in length, and four hundred feet in breadth at its widest part, being barely nine hundred yards in circumference. It is of an oval form, with an indentation at the southern end, where a stone wall has been built up from the rock to support the soil, and to protect it from the force of the current. For this purpose a sunk wall has been carried all round the island. The rock is wholly of granite, and the covering of earth is so light throughout, that the rock in many places projects above the soil. In several parts stairs lead down to the river.

The surface of this island is studded with superb ruins: by the natives it is called *Djeziret-el-Birbeh*, or the Island of Temples, — a very appro-priate appellation, since not fewer than eight temples, or sanctuaries, are crowded together on this small island. These temples do not appear to have been erected with any attention to symmetry; but the effect of the whole is most imposing. The principal edifices are approached by an avenue, formed on each side by a gallery supported by columns, the capitals of which are all different with respect to each other. There are thirty of these pillars on the left, and on the right only sixteen, with cells (probably for the habitations of the priests) within them. The greater part of these last-mentioned columns are finished, but the rest are incomplete. At the end of the avenue is a large pylon formed by two moles; the entrance in the centre has had two lions, and two small obelisks of red granite, before it. In all parts of the island, on the sides of the temples, are Greek inscriptions, commemorating the worship of Greek and Roman generals, who had come to pay their vows to Isis and Serapis. A French inscription on a stone in the entrance-way, engraved by the sculptor Castet, announces that this island was the southern

Pt. 5.

boundary of the temporary conquests of the French in Egypt, under Buonaparte. Twenty days after they landed at Alexandria, they discomfited and put the Mamelukes to flight at the battle of the pyramids, and drove them beyond the cataracts. This inscription is dated

" Le 13 Ventose, an 7 de la République, 3 Mars, an de J^s Cst 1799."

Philæ is said to have been the spot where the wrath of Isis was appeased for the violence which Typhon had offered to her husband Osiris; and hence we find so many temples dedicated to her in so small a compass, there being not less than four erected in honour of her, which must be seen, in order to form an adequate conception of their magnificence. From the figure of a cross having been discovered in one of the apartments of the principal temple (the remains of which appear in our engraving), it has been conjectured that this temple has been used as a Christian church.

Philæ is a rich field for the study of Egyptian art. The different buildings afford examples of the styles of its different æras, and the unfinished state of some of them throws light on the manner of their construction. It seems evident that the antient Egyptians were accustomed, first, to construct great masses, and afterwards to labour for ages in finishing the details of the decorations, beginning with the sculpture of hieroglyphics, and then passing on to stucco and painting. On one of the propyla, for instance, there are several inscriptions partly effaced by the outline of bas-reliefs which have been cut on them; and in the colonnades there are capitals in every stage of progress, from the first rude outline marked upon the stone, to the highest and most elaborate finish. The Greek inscriptions in different parts of the temples are innumerable, and comprise a period extending from the age of the Ptolemies until after the establishment of Christianity. Nothing, in short, is finished, but what is of the highest antiquity. This island is supposed to have been the burying place of Osiris, who was worshipped under the type of the sacred hawk.

It is impossible for a Christian traveller to contemplate the profusion of magnificent ruins with which this island abounds, without feelings of admiration and astonishment, and without calling to mind how literally the prophetic denunciation has been fulfilled :—" The idols of Egypt shall be moved " at the presence of Jehovah. (Isa. xix. 1.)

₊ Bochart, Geographia Sacra, lib. iv. c. 26. (Operum, tom. i. pp. 268, 269.) Carne's Letters from the East, pp. 143—145. Legh's Narrative of a Journey in Egypt, &c., pp. 51, 52. Irby's and Mangles' Travels, pp. 106—108. Dr. Richardson's Travels, vol. i. pp. 481—500. Fuller's Travels through some Parts of Turkey, pp. 223 —227. Madden's Excursions, vol. i. pp. 365—370.

Drawn by A.W. Callcott. R.A. from a sketch by C. Barry Esq.r Arch.t   Engraved by W. Finden.

MOUNT LEBANON.

AND THE RUINS OF BAALBEC.

"WILL A MAN LEAVE THE SNOW OF LEBANON WHICH COMETH FROM THE ROCK OF THE FIELD."

JEREMIAH XVIII. 14.

MOUNT LEBANON,

AND

THE RUINS OF BAALBEC.

Drawn by A. W. Callcott, from a Sketch made on the spot by Charles Barry, Esq.

The snow-capt summits of Lebanon are exhibited in this view as they overlook the splendid ruins of Baalbec. By its exceeding height, this mountain proves a conservatory for abundance of snow; which, thawing in the heat of summer, affords supplies of water to the rivers and fountains in the valleys below. In the time of Solomon the snow of Lebanon was used for the purpose of cooling wine in the summer (Prov. xxv. 13.); and it appears to have been employed in the same way in the time of Jeremiah, who has an allusion to it. (Jer. xviii. 14.)

Baalbec is supposed by Gesenius, and other biblical critics and commentators, to be either Baal-Gad, a town at the foot of Lebanon on the frontiers of Palestine (Josh. xi. 17. xii. 7. xiii. 5.), or Baal-Hamon, which place is mentioned in Sol. Song, viii. 11. Baalbec appears to have been the original name, which the Greeks translated into their language by Heliopolis, which means the same thing, viz. The City of the Sun: the Romans adopted the Greek name, and the word Baalbec is not to be found in any antient author. The language of the country, however, has preserved the original appellation, while the Greek and Roman translation has perished with their dominion. It stands in a delightful situation on the eastern verge, and near the head of the valley of Beka, which leads down in a south-west direction to Tyre, and opens by a narrow pass in an easterly direction upon the Orontes, communicating with Tadmor, Hamath, and Mesopotamia; and it must have been a great thoroughfare and depôt for trade, when Babylon and Nineveh, Tyre and Sidon, possessed the commerce of the world. The magnificence of its ruins sufficiently attest the antient splendour and opulence of Baalbec. The houses are completely overturned, and the stones lying in heaps; the walls remain, and are supposed by Dr. Richardson to have been about four miles in circumference.

The principal ruins of Baalbec occupy a position of considerable elevation above the surrounding village, which is formed entirely of massive substructions of masonry intersected by vaulted passages. Many of the stones of which this artificial acropolis is built are of prodigious size. In the western boundary wall, there are three stones adjoining each other, at a considerable height from the ground, each of which, upon an average, is about sixty feet in length, twelve feet in thickness, and twelve feet in breadth. In the north boundary wall are eleven stones adjoining each other,

Pt. 7.

varying from forty-five to fifty feet in length, six feet in thickness, and ten feet in breadth. Two ruined temples of extraordinary magnitude, with adjoining courts and propylæa, occupy the site of the acropolis, the principal approach to which, from the plain, was by an enormous flight of steps, vestiges of which still remain. The columns of the Great Temple, of which six only remain, are about seven feet in diameter, and fifty-five feet high; they are of the Corinthian order, and still support a portion of their entablature, which is elaborately carved, particularly the frieze, in which is a succession of bulls and lions in high relief. The smaller temple, commonly designated the Temple of the Sun, is in a much more perfect state as regards its external walls. Several of the columns, which are also of the Corinthian order, still remain erect; they are about six feet in diameter, and support an entablature of the same proportions and elaborate workmanship as that of the Great Temple. The principal entrance is highly enriched with arabesque and other sculpture. The interior is adorned with Corinthian columns partly engaged in the walls, and with two tiers of niches for statues in the intervening spaces. The architecture of the courts and propylæa are of the same character and elaborate workmanship as the Temples. Although these magnificent ruins bear undoubted evidence of their being a work of the Romans about the time of Antoninus Pius, there is reason to believe that a considerable portion of the substructions is of a much earlier date, probably of the time of the Jewish kings. "The stones," says Dr. Richardson, "are compact limestone, which is the common stone of the country; and the soil of age with which they are covered, compared with other parts of the building which are decidedly Roman, would warrant our referring them to the remote period of eight and twenty hundred years; the æra of Solomon king of Israel and Judah, who built Hamath and Tadmor in the desert. The second builders of this pile have built upon the foundations of the former building; and, in order that the appearance of the whole might seem to be of one date, they have cut a new surface upon the old stones. This operation has not been completely finished, and some of the stones remain half cut, exhibiting part of the old surface and part of the new; so that the different æras of the building are exemplified in the same stone."

The soil which surrounds the stately ruins of Baalbec is rich and well cultivated: the present population is about five hundred souls, the greater part of whom are Mohammedans; the remainder are Syrian and Greek Christians.

***** Dr. Richardson's Travels, vol. ii. pp. 502—509. Captains Irby's and Mangles' Travels, pp. 215, 216. Rae Wilson's Travels, vol. ii. pp. 147—151. But the most copious details respecting the remains of Baalbec, illustrated by measurements and with numerous engravings, will be found in Mr. Wood's splendid work on " The Ruins of Baalbec," published at London in 1753, and reprinted in 1827, with impressions from the original plates.

Drawn by J.M.W Turner; H.A from a sketch by Sir A.F.thurstone.

Engraved by W. Finden.

R A M A H.

With the building called Rachels Tomb.

In Ramah there was a voice heard, lamentation and weeping, Rachel
weeping for her Children.

MATT. II. 18. JER. XXXI. 15.

RAMAH

AND

THE TOMB OF RACHEL.

Drawn by J. M. W. Turner, from a Sketch made on the spot by the Rev. R. Master.

" A voice was heard in Ramah, lamentation *and* bitter weeping; Rachel weeping for her children."—
Jer. xxxi. 15.

RAMAH was a city allotted to the tribe of Benjamin (Josh. xv. 2, 3.), situated about six miles north of Jerusalem on the road to Bethlehem. From Judges, xix. 13. and Hos. v. 8. it should seem to have been not far from Gibeah. Here the prophet Samuel was born (1 Sam. i. 1.) and afterwards resided (ix. 18.): here he anointed Saul to be king over Israel (ix. 27. x. 1.), and finally was buried. (xxv. 1.) Though Ramah belonged to the tribe of Benjamin (Josh. xviii. 25.), yet it was included in the kingdom of Israel: as it stood in a pass between the kingdoms of Israel and Judah, Baasha king of Israel seized it, and began to fortify it, in order to prevent his subjects from passing by that way into the kingdom of Judah. (1 Kings, xv. 17. 21.) Here Nebuzaradan, the Chaldæan general, disposed of his Jewish prisoners after their capital was taken (Jer. xl. 1—3.); and as Rachel was buried in the vicinity of this place, she is in Jer. xxxi. 15. represented as come forth from her grave, and lamenting the loss of her children, who were either slain or gone into captivity.

The small square building surrounded by a dome or cupola, which is seen in our engraving, is called RACHEL's TOMB. Mr. Maundrell thinks that it may probably be the true place of her interment, mentioned in Gen. xxxvi. 19. But the present sepulchral monument cannot possibly be that erected by Jacob; for it is evidently a modern and Turkish structure, resembling in its exterior the tombs which are often raised to the memory of a Mohammedan santon or saint. Near this monument (the same traveller relates) is a small piece of ground, on which are

Pt. 12.

picked up little round stones, exactly resembling peas, concerning which there is a tradition that they once really were what they now seem to be, but that the blessed Virgin petrified them by a miracle, in punishment of a surly rustic, who denied her the charity of a handful of them to relieve her hunger.

*** Maundrell's Travels, p. 117.   Carne's Letters from the East, p. 277.

NO-AMMON, THEBES.

Portico of the great Temple at Karnak.

No shall be rent asunder.

EZEK XXX 16

Drawn by C. Stanfield, A.R.A. from a sketch by Major Felix.

Engraved by E. Finden.

NO-AMON. THEBES.

PORTICO OF THE GREAT TEMPLE AT KARNAK.

Drawn by C. STANFIELD, from a Sketch made on the spot by Major FELIX.

No, or No-Amon, or Amon of No (Jer. xlvi. 25. marginal reading), was the metropolis of Upper Egypt, by the Greek geographers termed Thebes, a city eminently distinguished for the worship of Jupiter, who by the Egyptians was called Amon or Ammon; hence the city received the appellation of Diospolis, or the city of Jupiter. The grandeur of antient Thebes must now be traced in the four small towns or hamlets of Luxor, Karnak, Medinet-Abou, and Gournou. Karnak is regarded by the most accurate modern travellers as the principal site of Diospolis; and the Egyptians seem to have called forth all the resources of wealth, and all the efforts of art, in order to render it worthy of their supreme divinity.

The great temple at Karnak, the principal portico of which is delineated in our engraving, has twelve principal entrances; each of which is composed of several propyla and colossal gateways, besides other buildings attached to them, in themselves larger than most other temples. One of the propyla is entirely of granite, adorned with the most finished hieroglyphics. On each side of many of them there have been colossal statues of basalt and granite, from twenty to thirty feet in height, some of which are in the attitude of sitting, while others are standing erect. A double range of colossal sphinxes extends across the plain from the temple at Luxor (a distance of nearly two miles), which terminates at Karnak in a most magnificent gateway, fifty feet in height, which still remains unimpaired. From this gateway the great temple was approached by an avenue of fifty lofty columns, one of which only now remains, leading to a vast propylon in front of the portico. The interior of this portico presents a *coup d'œil*, which surpasses any other that is to be found among the remains of Egyptian architecture. Twelve columns, sixty feet high, and of a beautiful order, form an avenue through the centre of the building, like the nave of a Gothic cathedral, and they are flanked on each side by sixty smaller ones, ranged in six rows, which are seen through the intervals in endless perspective. The walls are covered with bas-reliefs of a similar character with those found in the other antient Egyptian temples.

In an open space beyond the portico there were four obelisks, two only of which are now standing. One of these is seen in our engraving: according to Capt. C. F. Head, it has a base of eight feet square, and rises to a height of eighty feet, and is formed of a single block of granite. The hieroglyphics, which are beautifully wrought, are supposed to record the succession of Pharaohs who reigned over Egypt. From the most antient rulers of the land to the Ptolemies, almost every king, except the Persian, has his name recorded in this temple. But it was said, " the sceptre of Egypt shall depart away" (Zech. x. 11.); and, as if in direct fulfilment of the prophecy, the portion of the rocky tables that was to have been occupied by the names of others of its royal line, has been shattered, and (it has been conjectured) by no human hand.

The most interesting of the sculptured ornaments in this temple, Capt. Head states, are on the north-west, where there are battle-scenes, with innumerable figures of military combatants using bows and arrows, spears and bucklers, of prostrate enemies, of war chariots and horses. The fiery action and elegant shape of the steeds are remarkable. On the exterior walls of the south-west corner of the portico, are depicted other victories, which are conjectured to be those of the Egyptians over the Jews.

The field of ruins at Karnak is about a mile in diameter. Dr. Richardson conjectures that the whole of this space was once, in the prouder days of Thebes, consecrated entirely to the use of the temple. There are evidences of walls considerably beyond this, which probably enlarged the city in its greatest extent; but, after the seat of government had been withdrawn, the capital removed to another spot, and the trade transferred to another mart, the inhabitants narrowed the circuit of their walls, and placed their houses within the line of the sacred confines.

Such is the mass of disjointed fragments collected together in these magnificent reliques of antient art, that more than human power would appear to have caused the overthrow of the strong-holds of superstition. Some have imagined that the ruin was caused by the instantaneous concussion of an earthquake. Whether this conjecture be well founded or erroneous, the divine predictions against Egypt have been literally accomplished. " The land of Egypt" has been made " desolate and waste;" " judgments" have been executed " in No," whose " multitude" has been " cut off;" and NO IS RENT ASUNDER. (Ezek. xxix. 9. xxx. 14, 15, 16.)

₊ Fuller's Tour in some Parts of the Turkish Empire, pp. 186, 187. Capt. C. F. Head's Eastern and Egyptian Scenery, pp. 18, 19. Dr. Richardson's Travels, vol. ii. p. 96.

RUINS OF SELAH (PETRA).

TEMPLE EXCAVATED OUT OF THE ROCK.

Drawn by David Roberts, from a Sketch by the Count Léon de Laborde.

"Edom shall be a desolation : every one that goeth by it shall be astonished." —*Jer.* xlix. 17.

Selah is the name of a place mentioned in 2 Kings xiv. 7., where we read that Amaziah, king of Judah, " slew of Edom in the Valley of Salt ten thousand, and took Selah by war." As Selah in Hebrew signifies a rock, and corresponds with the Greek word Πετρα (Petra), geographers and commentators have reasonably inferred that the city bearing this name, and which was the celebrated capital of Arabia Petræa, is the place mentioned by the sacred historian. It is situated in the Ouadi (Wady) Mousa, or Valley of Moses, not far from Mount Hor : and the magnificent ruins which still remain, attest the antient splendour of that city. Our view exhibits a magnificent temple, cut out of the solid rock. The approach is through a gloomy winding passage, about two miles in length, the sides increasing in height as the path descends. Where the tops of the precipices are at the highest, a beam of stronger light breaks in at the close of the dark perspective, and the beautiful façade of the temple bursts upon the view of the astonished traveller.

" We know not," say Captains Irby and Mangles, by whom this edifice has been minutely described, " with what to compare this scene ; perhaps there is nothing in the world that resembles it. Only a portion of a very extensive architectural elevation is seen at first, but it has been so contrived that a statue with expanded wings, perhaps of Victory, just fills the centre of the aperture in front ; which, being closed below by the sides of the rock folding over each other, gives to the figure the appearance of being suspended in the air at a considerable height ; the ruggedness of the cliffs below setting off the sculpture to the highest advantage. The rest of the design opened gradually at every pace as we advanced, till the narrow defile, which had continued thus far without any increase of breadth, spreads on both sides into an area of moderate size ;" the naturally inaccessible sides of which present the same awful and romantic pictures as the avenues which lead to it.

The temple is of very lofty proportion, the elevation comprising two

Pt. 6.

stories. . . . No part is built, the whole being purely a work of excavation, and its minutest embellishments, wherever the hand of man has not purposely effaced and obliterated them, are in an admirable state of preservation. " There is, in fact, scarcely a building of forty years' standing in England, so well preserved in the greater part of its architectural decorations. Of the larger members of the architecture nothing is deficient, excepting a single column of the portico. Those on each side of the portico represent in groups, each of them, a centaur and a young man. This part of the work only is imperfect. In the upper tier the figures are females; two are winged, and two appear to have been dancing, or much in action, with some instruments lifted above their heads. The centre figure, which doubtless was the principal one, is too much defaced for her attributes to be determined; nor is there any thing in the ornaments that could enable us to discover to what divinity the temple had been dedicated."

The interior apartments, in the judgment of Captains Irby and Mangles, are comparatively small, and unworthy of so magnificent a portico. On the summit of the front is placed a vase, also hewn out of the solid rock, which the Arabs (by whom it is called *Hasnah-el-Faraoun*, or the Treasure of Pharaoh) imagine to be filled with the most valuable treasure. It exhibits in the numerous shot-marks on its exterior so many proofs of their cupidity; for it is so situated as to be inaccessible to other attacks. This temple has been admirably preserved from the ravages of time and the weather by the massive projection of the natural cliffs above. " The half pediments, which terminate the wings of the building, are finished at the top with eagles, which, combined with the style of architecture, differing little from the Roman, can leave no doubt that this great effort of art is posterior to the time of Trajan's conquest. . . . . The wide space which constitutes the area before the temple, is about fifty yards in width, and three times as long." It terminates to the south in a wild precipitous cliff, some of the heights of which are rendered accessible, though with great difficulty, by flights of steps which have been cut in them. Some small pyramids, likewise hewn out of the rock, are on the summits of these heights.

** Captains Irby's and Mangles' Travels in Egypt and Nubia, Syria, and Asia Minor, pp. 418—422.

Drawn by J. M. W. Turner R A from a sketch by Sir R Kerr Porter.

Engraved by J Cousen.

BABYLON.

"Her foundations are fallen, Her walls are thrown down, for it is the vengeance of the Lord." JEREM. L.15.

"Babylon shall become heaps — without an inhabitant." JEREM. LI. 37.

"Her pomp is brought down to the grave." ISAIAH XXI. 9.

BABYLON.

Drawn by J. M. W. TURNER, from a Sketch made on the Spot by
SIR ROBERT KER PORTER, Knight.

Babylon shall become heaps . . . . . without an inhabitant. — *Jer.* li. 37.

IF ever there was a city which seemed to bid defiance to any prediction of its fall, that city was " great Babylon" (Dan. iv. 30.), " the glory of kingdoms, the beauty of the Chaldees' excellency " (Isa. xiii. 19.), the " golden city " (Isa. xiv. 4.), " the lady of kingdoms " (Isa. xlvii. 5.). " abundant in treasures, ... the praise of the whole earth." (Jer. li. 13. 41.) For a long time, Babylon (which was one of the four cities said to have been founded by Nimrod) was the most·celebrated city in the whole world. Its massive walls, which were defended by two hundred and fifty towers, were reckoned among the wonders of the world, and appeared rather like the workmanship of nature than the bulwarks of man. " The temple of Belus, half a mile in circumference, and a furlong in height — the hanging gardens, which, piled in successive terraces, towered as high as the walls — the embankments, which restrained the Euphrates — the hundred brazen gates — and the adjoining artificial lake — all displayed many of the mightiest works of mortals concentrated in a single spot. Yet, while in the plenitude of its power, and, according to the most accurate chronologers, one hundred and sixty years before the foot of an enemy had entered it, the voice of prophecy pronounced the doom of the mighty . . . . . At a time when nothing but magnificence was around Babylon the Great, fallen Babylon was delineated exactly as every traveller now describes its ruins." *

It was foretold that God would stir up the Medes and Elamites (or Persians) against it (Isa. xxi. 2. Jer. li. 11.); that the river Euphrates should be dried up (Isa. xliv. 27. Jer. l. 38. li. 36.); and that the city should be taken by surprise during the celebration of a festival, when " her princes and her wise men, her captains and her rulers, and her mighty men should be made drunk. (Jer. l. 24. li. 39. 57.) All which was literally fulfilled when Belshazzar and his thousand princes, who were drunk with him at a great feast, were slain by the soldiers of Cyrus (men of various nations); after Cyrus had turned the course of the Euphrates, which ran through the midst of Babylon, and so drained off its waters, that the river became easily fordable for his soldiers to enter the city. Further, it was particularly foretold that God would " make it a possession for the *bittern* and *pools of water*" (Isa. xiv. 23.); which was accordingly realized by the country being overflowed, and becoming boggy and marshy, in consequence of the Euphrates being turned out of its course in order to take the city, and never restored to its former channel. This scene is thus described by the Hon. Major Keppel, who visited the ruins of Babylon in 1824 : — " As far as the eye could reach, the horizon presented a broken line of mounds. The whole of this place was a desert flat; the only vegetation was a small prickly shrub thinly scattered over the plain, and some patches of grass, where the water had lodged in *pools*, occupied by immense flocks of *bitterns*. †

The following passages from the Prophets Jeremiah and Isaiah graphically describe the critical situation of the once proud city of Babylon : — " The wild beasts of the desert shall dwell there, and the owls shall dwell therein; and it shall be no more inhabited for ever,

---

* Keith on the Fulfilment of Prophecy, p. 256. 8vo. edition.
† Journey from India to England, vol. i. p. 125.

neither shall it be dwelt in from generation to generation. As God over-threw Sodom and Gomorrah and the neighbour cities thereof, so shall no man dwell there, neither shall any son of man dwell therein. They shall not take of thee a stone for a corner, nor a stone for foundations; but thou shalt be desolate for ever, saith the Lord. — Babylon shall become heaps. . . . It shall never be inhabited, neither shall it be dwelt in from generation to generation; neither shall the Arabian pitch tent there, neither the shepherds make their fold there. But wild beasts of the desert shall lie there. (Jer. l. 39, 40. li. 26. 37. Isa. xiii. 20, 21.)

It is truly astonishing with what singular exactness these predictions (which are only a selection from many more which might have been adduced) have been fulfilled. After the capture of Babylon by Cyrus, it ceased to be a metropolis: and its final depopulation and ruin were completed by the erection of the new cities of Seleucia and Ctesiphon, which were built for this express purpose, in its neighbourhood, B. C. 293. Its desolation continues to this day. The whole face of the country is covered with vestiges of building, in some places consisting of brick-walls surprisingly fresh, in others merely a vast succession of mounds and rubbish, the greater part of which are certainly the remains of edifices, which were originally *disposed* in streets, and crossed each other at right angles. Three of these mounds, or hillocks, which are situated on the *eastern* bank of the Euphrates, are particularly worthy of notice, —

1. The HILL OF AMRAM, so called from the prophet of that name who is said to have been interred therein, is of an irregular form, and presents a great mass of bricks, mortar, and cement. From the summit of this eminence our view is taken. The river Euphrates is seen, flowing through the vast assemblage of ruins. In the centre is seen

2. The mass of ruins fitly termed MAKLOUBÉ, or, according to the vulgar Arabic pronunciation, MUJELIBÉ, that is, "*overturned.*" It is of an oblong, irregular shape, and its summit is covered with heaps of bricks and other rubbish. There are numerous caverns, which are now the refuge of jackals and other savage animals; and the king of the forest now ranges over the site of that Babylon which Nebuchadnezzar built for his own glory. All the ruins, indeed, abound with lions, and other wild beasts. Not an Arab nor a shepherd pitches his tent there.

3. The KASR, or Palace, appears to have been the most remarkable of the buildings erected in the eastern part of the city, and is conjectured to have been a relic of the celebrated hanging gardens. On the northern front of this ruin, upon an artificial pyramidal height, stands a solitary tree, of great celebrity among the Mohammedans: the natives call it ATHLEH, and assert that it flourished in antient Babylon, from the destruction of which they say that God preserved it, in order that it might afford Ali a convenient place to tie up his horse after the battle of Hellah. Captain Mignan states that it is the oriental tamarisk. It appears to be of the greatest antiquity, and it has been a superb tree, perhaps a scion of the monarch of the hanging gardens. Its present height, he adds, is only twenty-three feet: its trunk has been of great circumference, and, although nearly worn away, it still has sufficient strength to bear the burden of its evergreen branches, which, gently waving in the wind, produce a rustling, melancholy sound.

⁎ Sir R. K. Porter's Travels in Georgia, Persia, &c., vol. ii. pp. 308—332. 337—400.; Mr. Rich's Two Memoirs on the Ruins of Babylon; Hon. Major Keppel's Narrative of a Journey from India to England, vol. i. pp. 171—188. The accounts of these and of other subsequent travellers are digested into an admirable elucidation of the prophecies concerning Babylon, by the Rev. A. Keith, in his "Evidence of the Truth of the Christian Religion, derived from the Literal Fulfilment of Prophecy," pp. 255—338. 8vo. edition; Mignan's Travels in Chaldæa, pp. 183—185.

RUINED TEMPLE OF ISIS IN ETHIOPIA.

(At Ghertassey)

ISAIAH XVIII 1 XX 5

Drawn by A.W. Callcott R A from a sketch by C. Barry Esq

Engraved by E Finden

RUINED TEMPLE OF ISIS, IN ETHIOPIA

(AT GHERTASHER).

Drawn by A. W. Callcott, from a Sketch made on the spot by Charles Barry, Esq.

Ethiopia Proper, which comprises the modern countries of Nubia and Abyssinia, lying to the south of Egypt, is frequently mentioned in the Prophetic Writings in conjunction with the latter country. This is particularly the case in the denunciation against *both* countries in Isa. xx., Ezek. xxx. 1—20., and in Ezek. xxix. 10. (marginal rendering), in which last passage we read, " I will make Egypt waste from Migdol to Syene," or Assouan, on the confines of Ethiopia, which prediction was fulfilled by the invasion of Nebuchadnezzar: and the magnificent ruins which yet remain attest how literally Ethiopia has " fallen."

One of the most interesting memorials of antient art in this country, is the ruined Temple of Isis, at Ghertasher, which place is variously called Gortas, Gartaas, and Kardassy or Khardassy, by different travellers, who have endeavoured to transmit, by writing, the names of places as they were pronounced to them by the natives. The name Kardassy is applied to about six miles' extent of country, throughout which (Sir Frederick Henniker states) are visible the foundations of many buildings, that would, if completed, have rendered it a city of temples. The remains of the temple delineated in our engraving, are situated on the western bank of the Nile, not many miles above Assouan: they consist of six beautifully finished columns with enriched capitals. Two of them, facing the north, which are seen on the right hand of our view, are engaged in a wall two thirds of their height, forming a gateway; they have quadrangular capitals supported by the head of Isis, represented with cows' ears as at Denderah. The faces are well preserved, and have the peculiar form, the prominent eye, and soft expression of the lip, which generally characterise the Egyptian statues, and of which a living model may now and then be found among the Egyptian women of the present day. The other four columns, two on the west and two on the east, are also engaged in a wall half their height. The capitals vary, but are of the lotus form: two of them have the grape and wheat-ear in relief under their volutes. The columns stand on circular bases, and the foundation of the whole is partly seen. The architraves, entablature, and part of the cornice remain.

Pt. 7.

The shafts are about three feet in diameter, and about ten feet apart. The north front is thirty feet, the east and west is thirty-six feet. On a column of the north front are characters, much defaced, of a Greek inscription; on the other column are characters, none of which could be traced by Captain Light. A little to the north of these ruins are quarries of sandy freestone, containing not fewer than one hundred Greek inscriptions, with busts placed in the niches which are cut in the face of the rock. The purport of these inscriptions (which are of the æra of the Antonines) is, that the individuals named therein had come there to worship, and had presented offerings for themselves, their wives and children, and their friends.

₊ Light's Travels in Egypt, Nubia, the Holy Land, and Cyprus, pp. 57—60. In pp. 271. and following, Captain Light has given copies of five of the inscriptions above mentioned, with translations by Dr. Young. Captains Irby's and Mangles's Travels in Egypt, Nubia, &c., pp. 104, 105. These travellers, as well as Norden (Travels in Nubia, vol. ii. p. 130. 8vo edition), call Ghertasher Hindaw, which is the name of a spot further south, and which appears to be included in the district called Wady Khardassy. Burckhardt's Travels in Nubia, pp. 7, 8. 112, 113. Fuller's Tour in some Parts of the Turkish Empire, pp. 220, 221. Cooper's Egyptian Scenery.

EGYPT.

With a View of the Pyramids of Ghizeh.

LONDON.

Drawn by J. M. W. Turner. R.A. from a sketch taken on the spot by C. Barry. Esq.

Engraved by E. Finden.

EGYPT.

WITH A NEAR VIEW OF THE PYRAMIDS OF GHIZEH.

Drawn by J. M. W. Turner, from a Sketch made on the spot by Charles Barry, Esq.

EGYPT is a celebrated country in the north of Africa, at the eastern part of the Mediterranean Sea. By the Hebrews it is called Mizraim, which name it is supposed to have received from Mizraim, the son of Ham and grandson of Noah, by whom and his descendants it was originally peopled: of this name the Arabic appellation *Misr* is a contraction. By the Greeks and Romans it was called Ægyptus, whence the modern name of Egypt is derived; but its origin is unknown. The population of this country is computed to be less than three millions of inhabitants: its extent from Syene or Assouan to the Mediterranean Sea is about five hundred miles; its breadth is very unequal. In some places the inundations of the river Nile (of which an account is given in Part XXII.) extend to the foot of the mountains; in other parts there remains a strip of a mile or two in breadth, which the water never covers, and which is, therefore, always dry and barren. Egypt is usually divided into Upper and Lower: but antient writers speak of three divisions; viz. Upper Egypt or Thebais; Middle Egypt or Heptanomis; and Lower Egypt, including the Delta and the adjoining provinces. In modern times the Arabs have changed the classical appellation of Thebais into Said, or the high country; the Heptanomis into Vostani; and the Delta into Bahari, or the maritime district. In Upper Egypt the heat is often as great as it is under the equator: in Lower Egypt the climate is more temperate. Throughout the year, the dew is so heavy as to resemble gentle rain: in summer many diseases prevail; and of old there seem to have been some, of a dreadful nature peculiar to this land. (Deut. xxviii. 27.) The fertility of Egypt has been celebrated among antient nations; and at the present day there is no country more amply supplied with grain, fruits, and garden plants. In Lower Egypt oranges, dates, lemons, almonds, and plantains are very plentiful: flax continues to be cultivated. (Exod. ix. 31.) Egyptian cotton is well known in the commercial world; and maize or Indian corn, together with melons of various sorts, are also abundant.

The early history of Antient Egypt is involved in great obscurity. All accounts, however, and the results of modern researches, seem to concur in representing culture and civilisation as having been introduced and spread in Egypt from the south; and that the country in the earliest times was possessed by several contemporary kings or states, which at length were united into one great kingdom. The common name of the Egyptian kings was *Pharaoh*, which signifies sovereign power. History has preserved the names of several of these kings, and a succession of their dynasties: but the inclination of the Egyptian historians to magnify the great antiquity of their nation has destroyed their credibility. The recent researches of the learned in Egyptian hieroglyphics have enabled them to discover the names of several of the Pharaohs.

The revolutions and state of Egypt were minutely described by the prophets Isaiah, Jeremiah, and Ezekiel. Chap. xxxii. of the last-mentioned prophet is a sublime prediction of its fall, delivered in diversified and beautiful imagery: and in chapters xxix. 15. 10. and xxx. 6. 12, 13., among other denunciations, Ezekiel expressly says that " Egypt shall be the basest of kingdoms; neither shall it exalt itself any more among the nations: for I will diminish them, that they shall no more rule over the nations. I will make the land of Egypt utterly waste and desolate, from the tower of Syene even under the border of Ethiopia. The pride of her power shall come down: from the tower of Syene shall they fall in it by the sword. And I will make the rivers dry, and sell the land into the hand of the wicked; and I will make the land waste, and all that is therein, by the hand of strangers. I will also destroy the idols, and I will cause the idols to cease out of Noph" (or Memphis). It is now upwards of two thousand four hundred years since this prophecy was delivered; and the event has shown that, unlikely as it appeared when delivered, it has literally been fulfilled. For, not long afterwards, Egypt was successively attacked and conquered by the Babylonians and Persians: on the subversion of the Persian empire by Alexander, it became subject to the Macedonians; then to the Romans; and after them to the Saracens; then to the Mamelukes, and since their extirpation, to the Turks. Syene (or Assouan) is in ruins; and the idols of Egypt are scattered: from the neglect of the canals, which diffused fertility from the fecundating waters of the Nile, a large tract of country is abandoned to sand and to unfruitfulness, while the effect is a fulfilment of the threatening, " I will make her rivers dry;" and what was once a fruitful field has become desolate. Lately, indeed, Egypt has risen, under its present spirited but despotic pasha, to a degree of political importance and power unknown to it for many past centuries. Yet this fact, instead of militating against the truth of prophecy, may serve to illustrate another prediction; which implies that, however base and degraded it might continue to be throughout many generations, it would, notwithstanding, have strength sufficient to be looked to for aid or protection, even at the time of the restoration of the Jews to Judæa, who will seek " to strengthen themselves in the strength of Pharaoh, and trust in the shadow of Egypt." Other prophecies respecting it await their fulfilment: yet, whatever its present apparent strength may be, it is still but " the shadow of Egypt." (Isa. xxx. 2. xxxi. 1.) The whole earth shall yet rejoice, and Egypt shall not be for ever " base." (Compare Isa. xix. 19—25.)

The most extraordinary monuments of Egyptian power and industry were the PYRAMIDS, which still subsist to excite the wonder and admiration of the world. It has been supposed that they were erected by the Israelites, during their bondage in Egypt; but this supposition is contradicted by the tenor of antient history in general, as well as by the results of modern researches. Our engraving represents a near view of the Pyramids of Ghizeh, of which a distant view and general description were given in Part XXII. The second, in point of magnitude, is the Pyramid of Cephrenes, for the discovery of the interior of which we are indebted to the enterprising researches of the late Mr. Belzoni. On the authority of Herodotus, it had generally been believed that this pyramid contained no chambers: but Mr. Belzoni, suspecting from certain indications that an entrance might be found, set forty Arabs to work, to open the ground between the pyramid and part of a portico of a temple which stood before it. They soon came to the lower part of a large temple, reaching within fifty feet of its base: its exterior walls are formed of enormous blocks, some of them in the porticos being twenty-four feet in length. The interior is built of calcareous stones of various sizes, many of them finely cut at the angles. Mr. Belzoni thinks that it is probably much older than the exterior wall, which bears the appearance of as great antiquity as the pyramids. In order to find the basis of the pyramid on this side, and to ascertain whether any communication existed between it and the temple, he had to cut through large blocks of stone and mortar which rose forty feet from the basis. At length he came to a flat pavement cut out of the solid rock, which appears to run all round the pyramid. No other discovery was made on this side: but, on the north side, after sixteen days of fruitless labour, one of the Arabs perceived a chink between two stones, which led to the detection of a false entrance, that had evidently been forced. The upper part, however, had fallen in, and it was found impossible to penetrate beyond a hundred feet. But Mr. Belzoni did not despair of success: having strictly noticed the situation of the entrance of the first pyramid, he plainly perceived that it was not in the centre. He observed that the passage ran in a straight line from the outside of the pyramid to the east side of the king's chamber; which chamber being nearly in the centre of the pyramid, the entrance must consequently be as far from the middle of the face, as the distance from the centre of the chamber to the east side of it. This observation proved the right clue: on returning to the second pyramid, he was equally astonished and delighted to find the same marks which he had noticed on the other spot in the centre, and which had led him to make his first unsuccessful attempt about thirty feet distant from the spot where he stood. The discovery of the first granite stone occurred on the 28th of February, 1816; and on the 1st of March he uncovered three large blocks of granite. On the next day he came to the right entrance: it is a passage four feet high, three feet six inches wide, and descending towards the centre, for one hundred and four feet five inches, at an angle of twenty-six degrees. This passage was found to be lined with large blocks of granite; and, on clearing out the stones which had fallen down into it, the Arab labourers came to a fixed block of stone, which appeared to put an end to all further operations. Having on close inspection discovered that this immense block was, in fact, a portcullis of granite, one foot three inches thick, Mr. Belzoni contrived means to raise it; when he found himself in a passage similar in dimension, to the first, about twenty-two feet and a half in length. At the end of this is a perpendicular shaft of fifteen feet, which he descended by means of a rope, and then entered another passage running down at an angle of twenty-six degrees towards the north. He then ascended an inclined passage, which brought him to a horizontal one in the centre. After passing the portcullis, all the passages are cut out of the live rock. On advancing, the sides of the horizontal passage were found covered with arborizations of nitre, in various forms: at length he came to a door leading to a central chamber. This he entered, and found, towards the western end, buried in the floor, a sarcophagus of the finest granite, eight feet long, three feet six inches wide, and two feet three inches deep in the inside. It is surrounded with large blocks of granite, apparently intended to prevent its removal. Like the pyramid of Cheops, it is destitute of hieroglyphics. The lid was half removed: and, amid a great quantity of earth and stones, disclosed some bones, which, on being sent to London, were declared to be those of a bull, of the Egyptian deity Apis. This chamber was found to be forty-six feet three inches by sixteen feet three inches, and twenty-three feet and a half in height. It was cut out of the solid rock from the floor to the roof, which is composed of large blocks of limestone, forming a sort of pointed roof of the same slope as the pyramid itself. On the walls were observed many scrolls, executed with charcoal in unknown characters, and nearly imperceptible: they rubbed off into dust at the slightest touch: but the following inscription in Arabic was copied by a Copt, who attended Mr. Belzoni, and was translated for him by Mr. Salame. " The Master Mohammed Ahmed, lapicide, has opened them; and the Master Othman attended this (*opening*); and the King Alij Mohammed at first (*from the beginning*) to the closing up."

Other passages were afterwards explored; one of which, running with a descent of twenty-six degrees towards the west, led to a similar chamber, thirty-two feet by nine feet nine inches, and eight feet and a half long. It contained some small blocks of stone, and several unknown inscriptions. At the end of a horizontal passage were found the grooves of another portcullis; the granite block of which had been removed, and was lying amidst some rubbish near the spot. Passing this portcullis, the passage ascended towards the exterior base of the pyramid, forming apparently a second outlet.

The upper part of this pyramid of Cephrenes has still remaining on it a thick coating of mortar, which renders it extremely dangerous to ascend.

⁎ Belzoni's Narrative of Operations and Discoveries in Egypt and Nubia, pp. 260—280. (London, 1820, 4to.) Bishop Newton's Dissertations on the Prophecies, Diss. XII. Keith on Prophecy, pp. 350, 351. (8vo edition.) Dr. Edward Robinson's Dictionary of the Bible, *voce* Egypt. (Boston, 1833.) Madox's Excursions in the Holy Land, &c. vol. i. p. 114.

MOUNT LEBANON.

And the Convent of St Antonio.

HOSEA XIV. 5 6 7.

Drawn by J.M.W.Turner R.A.from a sketch by C.Barry Esq.ᵗ

Engraved by W.Finden.

MOUNT LEBANON,

AND

THE CONVENT OF SAINT ANTONIO.

Drawn by J. M. W. Turner, from a Sketch by Charles Barry, Esq.

Lebanon is a long chain of limestone mountains, extending from the neighbourhood of Sidon on the west, to the vicinity of Damascus eastward. By the Greeks and Latins they are termed Libanus, and by the natives Gibl Leban, or the White Mountain; most probably from the perpetual snow with which some part or other of them is covered throughout the year. This snow is now (as it antiently was, Prov. xxv. 13.) carried to the neighbouring towns for the purpose of cooling liquors. Petrified sea-shells and marine substances have been discovered in the mountain; and serpents of great length, together with several venomous reptiles, are also found there.

This mountainous chain is divided into two principal ridges, parallel to each other, the most westerly of which is known by the name of Libanus; and the opposite, or eastern range, by the appellation of Anti-Libanus; but this distinction is not recognised by the natives. On the loftiest summit of all, Dr. Clarke observed the snow lying, not in patches, but investing all the higher part with that perfectly white and smooth velvet-like appearance, which snow only exhibits when it is very deep. In the Old Testament, numerous allusions are made to Lebanon, from which the sacred writers derive glowing images and beautiful metaphors.

Lebanon is by no means barren; the mountains are almost all well cultivated, and well peopled. In many parts their summits are level, forming plains in which corn and all kinds of pulse are sown. They are watered by numerous cold flowing springs and rivulets, and by streams of excellent water, which diffuse freshness and fertility on all sides. Omitting for the present the far-famed cedars of Lebanon (of which a distinct view will be given), we may here state, that vineyards and plantations of mulberry, olive, and fig trees are cultivated on terraces formed by walls, which support the earth, and prevent it from being washed away by the rains from the sides of the acclivities. The soil of the declivities, and of the hollows which occur between them, is most excellent, and produces abundance of corn, oil, and wine; which is as much celebrated in the East in the present day, as it was in the time of the prophet Hosea, who particularly alludes to these articles of produce, and to the fragrant heights of Lebanon. (Hos. xiv. 5—7.)

Of the general aspect of this celebrated ridge of mountains, our engraving will enable the reader to form an accurate idea. Here, in a most retired situation, stands the Maronite Convent of Saint Antonio, of

Pt. 3.

Kozhaia (or, as Pococke terms it, of Casieeh): it is erected on the spot where that reputed saint is said to have spent a part of his life in solitary meditation. It contains seventy or eighty resident friars; and some more austere brethren, who prefer to imitate the ascetic life of their patron saint, are lodged in lonely cells and hermitages in the cliffs which rise above it. This place is celebrated for its excellent wine, which is preserved in long earthen jars, stopped closely down with clay, as is usual in these parts of the East; but, being sent to distant places in skins, it acquires from them a strong disagreeable flavour. Dr. Pococke saw the friars standing in their church (which is excavated in the rock), four and four at two square desks, chanting their hymns alternately, and leaning on crutches to obtain some ease, during the long time they are required to spend in their devotions. At other times, being far removed from any town, they are compelled to perform every thing for themselves: hence, there are to be found among them carpenters, shoemakers, and every class of artificers which their simple mode of life requires. Some of them are employed in cultivating the lands belonging to the convent; and others, in an extensive printing establishment which has for many years been attached to it, and from which the neighbouring Christians are supplied with missals and other prayer books, legends of saints, religious tracts, and such portions of the Scriptures as are not withheld from the laity by the Romish church. They are well printed, on paper sent from Venice, in the Carshoon, that is, the Arabic language in Syriac characters, which the generality of the people comprehend.

The monks of Saint Antonio still pretend to the miraculous power of exorcising and casting out devils; and, as the popular belief gives full credit to their pretensions, maniacs are continually brought to them for cure. The scene of their thaumaturgic operations is a large grotto excavated in a cliff which overhangs the convent. In this dark and gloomy cavern the patient is heavily chained, and supplied with very scanty fare; a priest remains constantly near him, reciting certain forms of prayer; and he is, from time to time, drenched with cold water poured over him from buckets. This rude discipline is often successful. The patients are commonly brought to their senses in three or four days or a week, and rarely continue longer; and sometimes they are said to be cured while on their way to the convent. If, however, this treatment should eventually fail, the monks find a ready excuse for their want of success, by ascribing it to the patient's incredulity.

The monks of Saint Antonio are interred in a vault above ground, in their habits, in which they appear like skeletons; Dr. Pococke saw one, — a reputed holy man, — whose skin seemed to be uncorrupted.

*** Pococke's Description of the East, vol. ii. part ii. p. 103.; Richardson's Travels, vol. ii. p. 507.; Fuller's Tour through some Parts of the Turkish Empire, pp. 376, 377.; Rae Wilson's Travels, vol. ii. p. 103—108.; Dr. Clarke's Travels, vol. iv. pp. 201, 202.; Light's Travels, p. 219.

Drawn by J. D. Harding from a sketch taken on the spot by M.rs Bracebridge.

Engraved by E. Finden.

THE CEDARS OF LEBANON.

PSALM XXIX. 5.

DISTANT VIEW

OF

THE CEDARS OF LEBANON.

Drawn by J. D. HARDING, from a Sketch made on the spot by Mrs. BRACEBRIDGE.

IN Part XIII. a near view was given of the majestic Cedars of Lebanon.
together with historical notices of these justly celebrated trees. The
present engraving exhibits a distant view of the whole group: the trees
form a dark cluster in the centre, behind which rises the snow-clad
Lebanon, broken into fine bold sweeps. The stony fragments, seen in
the foreground, are of grey limestone, which is crumbled into small
detached masses. A group of Arabs was on the spot at the time this
view was taken. The Scriptures contain frequent references to the
fountains, wells, and streams of Lebanon, as well as to its cedars and
other trees. To those who are acquainted with the local scenery of
the tract where they are found, the allusions of the prophets appear very
striking. " We learn from Hosea (xiv. 7.) that Israel shall one day be
as the ' wine of Lebanon ;' and its wine is still the most esteemed of any
in the Levant. What could better display the folly of the man who had
forsaken his God, than the reference of Jeremiah (xviii. 14.) to the ' cold
flowing waters ' from the ices of Lebanon, the bare mention of which
must have brought the most delightful associations to the inhabitants of
the parched plain? The psalmist (xxix. 5.) declares that ' the voice of
the Lord breaketh the cedars ; yea, the Lord breaketh the cedars of
Lebanon : ' and a more sublime spectacle can scarcely be conceived, than
the thunder rolling among these enormous masses, and the lightning
playing among the lofty cedars, withering their foliage, crashing the
branches that had stood the storms of centuries, and with the utmost ease
hurling the roots and trunks into the distant vale. But by Isaiah the
mountain is compared to one vast altar, and its countless trees are the
pile of wood, and the cattle upon its thousand hills, the sacrifice ; yet, if
a volcanic eruption were to burst forth from one of its summits, and in
torrents of liquid fire to kindle the whole at once, even this mighty
holocaust would be insufficient to expiate one single crime ; and the

sinner is told, that ' Lebanon is not sufficient to burn, nor the beasts thereof for a burnt offering.' (Isa. xl. 16.) The trees of Lebanon are now comparatively few, and with them are gone the eagles and wild beasts, to which they afforded shelter; and it is of its former state, and not of its present degradation, that we are to think, in reading the glowing descriptions of the prophets. — ' The glory of Lebanon shall come unto thee, the fir-tree, the pine-tree, and the box together, to beautify the place of my sanctuary, and I will make the place of my feet glorious.' (Isa. lx. 13.) "

*** Hardy's Notices of the Holy Land, pp. 272, 273.   MS. Memorandum of Mrs. Bracebridge.

Drawn by D. Roberts, from a sketch by the Revᵈ R. Master.   TOMB OF ST JAMES.   Engraved by W. Finden.

BROOK KIDRON.   TOMB OF ABSALON.   TOMB OF ZACHARIAH.

THE VALLEY OF JEHOSHAPHAT.

Between Mount Moriah and the Mount of Olives.   JOEL. III. 2. 12.

THE VALLEY OF JEHOSHAPHAT,

BETWEEN

MOUNT MORIAH AND THE MOUNT OF OLIVES.

Drawn by D. ROBERTS, from a Sketch made on the spot by the Rev. R. MASTER

THE VALLEY OF JEHOSHAPHAT is a narrow but deep valley, situated a short distance to the east of Jerusalem; it is supposed to have derived its name from Jehoshaphat king of Judah being buried here. It is also called the VALLEY OF THE KEDRON, because the brook Kedron flows through it; and THE VALLEY OF DECISION in Joel, iii. 2. 12. 14., where we are informed that the Almighty will gather all nations in it, in order to be judged. The Mohammedans have a tradition that, at the last day, Mohammed will be seated on a pillar erected in this valley.

The valley of Jehoshaphat runs from north to south, between the Mount of Olives and Mount Moriah. On the left of our engraving flows the brook Kedron, of which an account has already been given in Part I., The edifice next to it is the tomb of Absalom, also delineated and described in the same Part. The tomb in the centre bears the name of Saint James: it is a plain cave, with the frieze of the portico sculptured, and supported by four round columns, so that it resembles the front of a small Grecian temple. The last tomb, seen on the right of our engraving, bears the name of Zechariah: like that of Absalom, its base is quadrangular, insulated from the parent rock, and adorned with Ionic pilasters; but, instead of metopes and triglyphs, a heavy projecting architrave runs round it, above which rises a smooth pyramid of masonry work. Whether these are really the sepulchres of those to whom they have been assigned, it is now impossible to determine: they evidently display an alliance of Egyptian and Grecian taste. The mixture of Grecian architecture unquestionably argues a later age. An intelligent anonymous modern traveller suggests that the reproof of the Pharisees by Jesus Christ, related in the latter part of the twenty-third chapter of Saint Matthew's Gospel, may serve to reconcile the manifest discrepancy between the style of these monuments and the period to which tradition refers them. " Our Saviour, then upbraiding the Pharisees with being actuated by the same unbelieving and perse-cuting spirit, that had impelled their fathers to shed the blood of the

Pt. 24.

prophets, though hypocritically pretending to revere the memories of those servants of God, uses these words: — ' Woe unto you, scribes and Pharisees, hypocrites, because ye build the tombs of the prophets, and *garnish* the sepulchres of the righteous;' and then declares that upon them should ' come all the righteous blood shed upon the earth from the blood of righteous Abel to the blood of Zacharias the son of Barachias' (Matt. xxiii. 29. 35.) ; as if the tomb of the latter had been in his mind at the time and suggested the reproach. According to this supposition, the base, hewn from the rock, possessing the character of that massive sepulchral architecture which the Israelites derived from Egypt, might very well have been the tombs of those to whom they are assigned, while the Ionic pilasters and other ornaments of a subsequent period might, not improbably, have been the garnishing of the sepulchres of the righteous alluded to by our Saviour, added either in his days or a short time before, when the reduction of Judea into a Roman province and the example of Herod had introduced a different style."

From a very early period, the narrow valley of Jehoshaphat has served as a burial place for the inhabitants of Jerusalem ; as we may infer from the account of the destruction of idolatry in Judah, and of the vessels made for Baal, when the bones of the priests of Baal were burnt to ashes at the brook Kedron, and were cast upon the graves of the children of the people. (1 Kings, xiii. 2. 2 Kings, xxiii. 6. 2 Chron. xxxiv. 4.) The Hebrew population of modern Jerusalem still inter their dead in this valley. Numerous tomb-stones are observable here : and as a strong inclination exists among the Jews, to have their remains entombed in the country of their ancestors, many of them arrive here with this view, in the course of the year, from the most distant lands. When Mr. Rae Wilson inquired the motive which prompted them to go to Jerusalem, the answer was — " To die in the land of our fathers." One day in the year, the Jews purchase from their Mohammedan oppressors permission to assemble in the Valley of Jehoshaphat, which time they pass in weeping and mourning over the desolation of Jerusalem, and their protracted captivity. It was on this side that the city was taken by assault by the besiegers in the first crusade.

. Chateaubriand, Itinéraire de Paris à Jérusalem, pp. 193—195. (Londres, 1832.) Rae Wilson's Travels, vol. i. pp. 216—220. Three Weeks in Palestine, pp. 39. 42—44. Hardy's Notices of the Holy Land, &c. pp. 167, 168.

E D O M .

Triumphal Arch across the Ravine which forms one of
the approaches to Selah or Petra.

"Edom shall be a desolate Wilderness."
JOEL III. 19.

EDOM. — TRIUMPHAL ARCH

ACROSS THE RAVINE WHICH FORMS ONE OF THE APPROACHES TO SELAH OR PETRA.

Drawn by C. STANFIELD, from a Sketch made on the spot by Count LÉON DE LABORDE.

OF the striking scene delineated in this engraving, the enterprising traveller, who has contributed it, must speak for himself.

" Our conductor preceded us, calling our attention to some large slabs, traces of an antient pavement, by which the labour of man had converted this abrupt and wild ravine into a magnificent avenue. After many windings in the midst of this almost subterranean street (so near do the summits of the rocks above approach each other), we were arrested by a prospect which it were vain to attempt to describe. Our view is taken from the entry of the ravine. Two Arabs, with their camels, are seen in the foreground, advancing towards the city of Selah or Petra, the magnificent ruins of which, seen in the distance, fully exemplify the prophetic denunciation — ' Edom shall be a desolation.' (Joel, iii. 19.) A grand triumphal arch raised at this spot, such as the antients were accustomed to construct at the approaches of cities, boldly connects together these two great walls of rocks. The impression produced by it is very imposing, at the moment the traveller enters this kind of covered way."

The novel disposition of this triumphal arch led M. de Laborde at first to think that it might have served, both as a passage from one side of the rocks to another, and also as a channel for conveying part of the waters of an aqueduct, which was carried along the ravine. He ascended by a steep opening incumbered with rocks; but after reaching the summit with difficulty, he found nothing which could authorise the supposition that this arch was destined for any other use, than that of adorning the approaches to the capital of Arabia Petræa.

Two other views of the ruins of Selah or Petra will be found in Parts VI. and VIII. of this work.

*** Voyage de l'Arabie Petrée, par MM. de Laborde et Linant, p. 58.

Pt. 15.

DAMASCUS.

I will break also the bar of Damascus. · AMOS 1 5

Drawn by A.W. Callcott. R.A. from a sketch by C. Barry Esq.ʳ

Engᵈ ʳᵉᵈ by E. Finden.

DAMASCUS.

Drawn by A. W. Callcott, from a Sketch made on the spot by Charles Barry, Esq.

" I will break also the bar of Damascus." — *Amos*, i. 5.

DAMASCUS ranks as a city of high antiquity; if, indeed, it be not the oldest city on the globe: it is first mentioned in Gen. xiv. 15. It stands on the river Barrady (the Chrysorrhoas or Golden Stream of the antient geographers), in a beautiful and most fertile plain, on the east and south-east of Anti-Libanus, open to the south and east, and bounded on the other sides by the mountains. The region around it, including probably the valley between the ridges of Libanus and Anti-Libanus, is in the Old Testament called Syria of Damascus or Demesk, and by Strabo, Cœlesyria. This city, which originally had its own kings, was taken by David (1 Sam. viii. 5, 6.), and subsequently by Jeroboam II. king of Israel. (2 Kings, xiv. 28.) Afterwards it was subject to the Assyrians, Babylonians, Persians, the Seleucidæ, and the Romans. In the time of Saint Paul it appears to have been held by Aretas, king of Arabia Petræa, the father-in-law of Herod Antipas. (2 Cor. xi. 32, 33.) At this period it was so much thronged by Jews, that according to Josephus (War, book ii. ch. xx. § 2.) ten thousand of them, by command of Nero, were put to death at once.

Modern Damascus, by the natives called *El Sham* (an appellation of uncertain meaning), though often captured and several times demolished, has always risen again to splendour and dignity, and has in all ages been mentioned as one of the finest and most delightful situations in the world: it may be called the Florence of Turkey, and the flower of the Levant. Surrounded with orchards planted on the beautiful and fertile plain of the Barrady, its situation has been celebrated with enthusiasm by oriental writers, who rank the Valley of Damascus first of the four terrestrial paradises. It is two miles in length from north-east to south-west; but its breadth is not in proportion, being extremely narrow, and it is divided into twenty-three districts. It appears formerly to have been inclosed within three strong walls, the destruction of which is announced by the prophets Jeremiah (xlix. 27.) and Amos. (i. 4, 5.) The first or innermost was the greatest in point of elevation, between which and the second was a ditch, and the third or exterior wall was the lowest. These walls had towers, some in a circular form, and others square. Mr. Rae Wilson considers the present wall, which is low and does not inclose it more than two thirds round, as standing on the site of the antient inner wall; the others being broken down, and the ditches full of rubbish. During the crusades, the eastern part was accounted impregnable. For a short time, under the Ommiade dynasty, Damascus was the capital of the Saracen empire or khalifate: it is now the capital of a pashalik of the Ottoman empire.

The streets are narrow, in order to shade the inhabitants from the heat of the sun. The houses are constructed with mud: few of them have floors of wood, or are provided with windows. In building them, the plan is to fix nails or pins of wood in the walls while they are soft, in order to suspend domestic articles thereon, as, from the frail material with which these walls are made, they would not admit the operation of a hammer. The roofs are flat like a terrace, and are spread over with a

Pt. 12.

kind of plaster, made firm with a roller. Many of them are surrounded with mud walls or battlements four feet in height, to prevent accidents. The better class of houses are spacious and elegant; the entrances to all, indeed, are bad, the doors of most being so small and low as to oblige the person entering to stoop. Within there is generally a quadrangular well-paved court, containing a stone or marble tank for water, and sometimes ornamented with plants, and a fountain of water. During great heats a kind of awning or veil is spread over the top of these courts. Every man's house is his castle; and in case of an irritated mob attacking any of its oppressors, he can shut himself up in his habitation, and remain till the governing power send a force to protect him.

The total population of Damascus is estimated at 150,000 souls, of whom a small proportion only is composed of Jews there are about 12,000 Christians of different sects and denominations. The remainder are Mohammedans. The Franciscan monks have a convent which bears the name of Saint Paul, the scene of whose miraculous conversion (related in the ninth chapter of the Acts of the Apostles) is pointed out to the Christian traveller, about a quarter of a mile from the eastern gate of the city: it is marked out by heaps of gravel and earth, and on the 25th day of January annually, in commemoration of this event, the Christians in Damascus walk in procession, and read the history of the apostle's conversion, under the protection of a guard furnished to them by the pacha. Not far from this spot, the part in the wall is also shown from which Paul was let down by night in a basket (after the manner of Rahab in the case of the spies, Josh. ii. 15.), in order to avoid the fury of the persecuting Jews who watched at the gate to kill him on account of his change of principles. (Acts, ix. 25.) At a small distance is exhibited the place where he rested, till some of his friends joined him in his flight.

The house of Judas, in which Ananias restored sight to the apostle (Acts, ix. 17.), is a small grotto or cellar, containing a Christian altar and a Turkish praying place. The street in which this house stands, and which is called "Straight" in Acts, ix. 11., forms the principal thoroughfare in this city: it is about half a mile in length, running from east to west; but as it is narrow, and the houses project into it in several places on both sides, it is difficult to form a clear idea of its length and straightness.

The zeal of the early Christians founded churches at Damascus; and a magnificent cathedral, which was dedicated to Saint John the Baptist (whose head is *said* to be deposited here), is now converted into a mosque. It is a noble edifice, six hundred and fifty feet in length, and one hundred and fifty in breadth, and has a large and beautiful marble court with a tank of water, and granite columns of the Corinthian order, supporting arches, the upper ones being half the height of the lower, and forming a double cloister. No Christian is permitted to enter this building. The other mosques are numerous, but in point of splendour are not to be compared with those of Constantinople.

Our engraving will enable the reader to form a general idea of this celebrated city: it is taken from the tomb of a Turkish santon or saint, situated on the plain in which Damascus stands.

⁎ Maundrell's Travels, pp. 164—180. Dr. Richardson's Travels, vol. ii. pp. 460—496. Rae Wilson's Travels, vol. ii. pp. 115—134. Carne's Letters from the East, pp. 374—386. Madox's Excursions in the Holy Land, &c. vol. ii. pp. 123—131.

89

Drawn & Sketched by the Hon. W. E. Fitzmaurice.

Engraved by E. Finden.

JAFFA THE ANTIENT JOPPA.

From the Sea.

JAFFA.

THE ANTIENT JOPPA.

Drawn by the Hon. Capt. W. E. Fitzmaurice.

JOPPA, called also Japha, and now universally Jaffa, is one of the most antient sea-ports in the world. It belonged to the tribe of Dan. (Josh. xix. 46.) Hither Solomon commanded the timber, hewn in Lebanon for the temple, to be brought, previously to its being carried to Jerusalem. (2 Chron. ii. 16.) At this port the prophet Jonah embarked for Tarshish, when he was commanded to preach repentance to the inhabitants of Nineveh. (Jonah, i. 3.) Here also Peter raised Tabitha from the dead (Acts, ix. 36—42.): and in 1831 a fragment of an antient wall, in the British vice-consul's house, was gravely asserted to be a relic of the identical dwelling of " one Simon, a tanner, whose house was by the sea-side." (Acts, x. 6.) On the destruction of Jerusalem by the Romans, many Jews retired here to defend themselves, but in vain ; for the place was besieged, captured, and destroyed, and twelve thousand Jews were put to death. In the time of the crusades, Joppa became the scene of great military enterprises. Here " Richard Cœur de Lion astonished the Saracens by his acts of valour, attacking them with the fury of a lion, and chasing them to Ramah, about twelve miles distant. In revenge for this repulse, in 1193 the Saracens stormed Joppa, and put twenty thousand of the inhabitants to the sword. Louis IX., king of France, rebuilt the walls at a vast expense, and erected towers in the year 1250 : these were afterwards destroyed, and the city itself nearly reduced to a mass of ruins. It revived, however, by degrees. In 1771 it suffered severely by a siege from Ali Bey, and from Mohammed Abudahal in 1776 ; and it was ultimately taken by the French on the 6th of March, 1799." The scene of the massacre of the Turkish prisoners, by order of Buonaparte, after the surrender of El Aresch, is yet pointed out to travellers. It was on the beach to the south of Jaffa. Four thousand prisoners (Barbaresques, that is, natives of Algiers, Tunis, and other towns on the Barbary coast, who had been sent to the aid of Djezzar Pacha,) were murdered in cold blood, having surrendered upon the promise of quarter. The plea alleged in excuse by Buonaparte was, that

Pt. 23.

they had previously been prisoners of war, but had been liberated on their parole, which they had broken. The truth of the poisoning of a number of his sick French troops has been attested by Signor Damiani, the British consul in 1831, though the number who thus perished has been greatly exaggerated.

Modern Jaffa is situated on a promontory, which rises about one hundred and fifty feet above the level of the Mediterranean Sea; it is now, as it antiently was, the principal port of Judæa, with reference to Jerusalem, whence it is distant about forty or forty-five miles to the north-west. As a station for vessels, its rocky harbour is one of the worst on the Asiatic coast. From its elevated situation, this town commands varied and picturesque prospects on every side. Towards the west is extended the open sea; towards the south are spread fertile plains, reaching as far as Gaza; towards the north, as far as Mount Carmel, the flowery meads of Sharon present themselves; and towards the east the hills of Ephraim and Judah raise their towering heads. The town is walled round on the south and east, towards the land; and partially so on the north and west, towards the sea.

The approach to Jaffa is destitute of interest. The town, of which our engraving conveys an accurate idea, from its situation on a promontory, and facing chiefly to the northward, looks like a heap of buildings crowded as closely as possible into a given space; and from the steepness of its site they appear to stand one upon another. The interior of the town corresponds with its outward mien, and has all the appearance of a poor village. The streets are very narrow, uneven, and dirty: the population is computed to be between four and five thousand, the greater part of whom are Turks and Arabs; the Christians are stated to be about six hundred, consisting of Romanists, Greeks, Maronites, and Armenians. The Greeks, Latins, and Armenians, have each a small convent for the reception of pilgrims. All the gardens in the neighbourhood abound with orange and lemon trees; there are also various other fruit trees. On the invasion of the French, among other acts of violence, they laid waste almost every garden. The different European powers have each their representative consul here, whose office is principally to assist the pilgrims to Jerusalem.

₊ Rae Wilson's Travels, vol. i. pp. 164—174. Three Weeks in Palestine, pp. 6 —10. Hardy's Notices of the Holy Land, pp. 128, 129. Dr. Richardson's Travels, vol. ii. pp. 208. 215, 216. Dr. Clarke's Travels, vol. iv. pp. 441—443.